DECEMBER 2021

AN ANTHOLOGY OF ARTICLES

BRAIN BOOSTER ARTICLES

ISBN 979-888555647-7

Contents

Preface

"Start writing, no matter what. The water does not flow until the faucet is turned on".

- Louis L'Amour

This book is a bouquet of articles contributed by students, professors and academicians. Hundreds of students and professors are contributing their work to Brain Booster Articles, we are here to provide ample information about Law and Contemporary issues. Our aim is to provide a platform for today's generation to express their views and ideas on law and contemporary law.

CHAPTER ONE

PANCHATANTRA AND NATURAL LAW SCHOOL OF JURISPRUDENCE

Author: Apeksha GM, II year of B.A.,LL.B. from Ramaiah College of Law

Abstract

Natural law can be easily understood as a philosophy that focuses on the laws of nature. It has been incessantly dominated the spheres of politics, legal, religion, social philosophy for ages now and continues to do so. Natural law is said to be a set of unwritten laws which contain the principles that are revealed by the nature of man or reason or are said to be derived from god himself[1].

Natural law represents a belief that there are a set of morals, ethics, ethos, and principles that are universal to the human race. They go beyond cultural, and regional differentiation and is common to all societies.[2]The philosophy behind natural law indicates that law is rational and reasonable, it put forths that laws are the logical evolution of morals, therefore morally wrong actions are wrong against the law[3].

Eg 1: Being loyal is moral. If A the husband cheats on B his wife then by being disloyal to her, then he is liable for the charges of adultery.

Eg 2: Not to destroy another's property is moral. If A in a fit of anger goes ahead and breaks the glasses of BMTC buses on the road he can be charged under the penal code for destroying public property.

In the next few pages, I have discussed how facets of natural law are evident in Indian Culture.

Ancient India's Concept to Deliver the Lessons of Morals

India as a country has always deemed morals with great esteem and reverence. A glance of the same can be witnessed in the Bhagavad Gita. The

Bhagavad Gita is centred on the moral dilemma that is faced by despondent Arjuna (one of the Pandavas) amid the battlefield. Lord Krishna is Arjuna's charioteer on the battlefield but essentially his spiritual guide. Just when the battle is about to begin, Arjuna is burdened with severe self-doubt about what he is just about to engage in: a bloody war with his cousins over a kingdom! His dilemma is whether it is appropriate for him to kill his own cousins Kauravas and other close associates for the sake of the kingdom, despite it being his legitimate claim. It is then that Lord Krishna enlightens him through the teachings that together form the Bhagavad Gita.[4]The main intention of these teachings is to help humans, with the task, which is, perhaps the most difficult, that is, to discriminate, choose and perform actions that are moral and righteous. One of the teachings of the Bhagavad Gita is that "tasmadasaktahsatatamkaryam karma samacaraasaktohyacaran karma param apnotipurushah"[5] which translates into "Therefore, without being attached to the fruits of activities, one should act as a matter of duty, by working without attachment one attains the Supreme"[6]. Arjuna finally decides to fight the Kauravas. However, it was not because he did not like them for cheating on him and his brothers. It was because that was the most logical course of action based on his Dharma (morality) demanded that by fighting the Kauravas and defeating them, he would ensure that justice had been delivered.

Though the concept of explaining morals with a storyline, a hero, a villain, and a guardian seems to be pretty impeccable, it couldn't be understood by all, the reason being the complexity of the verses, the language barrier as in earlier age the Gita was available in Sanskrit the language of the priestly class and the ruling class, it was neither understood nor transmitted to the commoners, and oral tradition being the most prevalent form to the transmission of epics and scriptures those days, the expanse of the Gita made it difficult to remembered and people also gave the Gita their renditions as time passed on. So there arose a need for a simple way of delivering morals to all ages and strata in the society, to build up a noble, righteous and virtuous society. This responsibility was put on the shoulders of the Panchatantra Stories, Jataka Tales, Janapada Stories, and many more short stories with important morals. Here in this article, we are going to discuss the prevalence of Panchatantra Tales in instilling moral values in we Indians.

Panchatantra

The Panchatantra is an ancient Indian collection of interrelated animal fables in Sanskrit. The word "Panchatantra" is a combination of two words Pancha- meaning five and Tantra- meaning the art to weave in Sanskrit. Translated into interweaving the five skeins and traditions and teachings into a text. The earliest recorded version of the Panchatantra is credited to Vishnu Sharma, dates back to 300 BCE. But these fables are likely much older, having been passed down by oral generation for ages.

Panchatantra was written to be a textbook for niti, i.e., "policy," especially for kings and statesmen; the maxims, proverbs, aphorisms, and adages tend to glorify shrewdness and cleverness rather than altruism. [7]

The story of why the Panchatantra came into existence is quite interesting. Once there was a ruler named Sudarshan, who had three sons. Though the king was quite intelligent and powerful, his sons were not a source of pride to him. The sons had no inclination or ability to learn anything. They were quite unimaginative, slow, and rather stupid. In desperation, the king turned to his counsellors for advice. One of his ministers, Sumati, seemed to make sense to Sudarshan. Sumati told the king that the task of educating the princes in the fields of politics, diplomacy, and the sciences can be handed over to Vishu Sharma, an aged scholar. The king wasted no time in inviting Vishnu to court and offered him a hundred land grants if he could turn the princes into learned scholars. Vishnu refused the gift, saying he did not sell knowledge and that he would take on the task and within six months make the princes wise so they would be able to rule as wisely as their father. Now, the method Vishnu devised was to gather and adapt ancient stories that had been told in India since time immemorial. He then created an interesting, entertaining work of five parts which he called the Five Principles and that became the Panchatantra. The princes learned the Five Principles and became wise, and the king was very pleased.[8]

The Five Sections of the Panchatantra

The Panchatantra has five parts or treatise and they deal with many nitis or morals. They are listed as follows

1. Mitra-bheda is the foremost principle of the Panchatantra, it translates into 'The Separation of Friends'. These stories are based on the conversation and interaction of Lions and Bulls, and the differences between them
2. Mitra-labha or Mitra-sampraptithe second principle translates into "The Gaining of Friends". These stories are based on the interaction and

conversation of Dove, Crow, Mouse, Tortoise, and Deer and the similarities between them.

3. Kakolukiyam which translates into Crows and Owls speaks volumes about war and peace in society.
4. Labdhapranasam translates into Loss Of Gains. Have stories based on The Monkey and the Crocodile and the facades each one plays to trick the other.
5. Apariksitakarakam, the last book is all about Ill-Considered Action/ Rash Deeds. It has stories where the leads are played by the Brahman and the Mongoose, and the light is thrown on how miscommunication, misinterpretation, decisions made in a fit of anger, or actions done with a malafide reason can lead to the greatest of losses in life.

These five principles (or five books) are a succession of animal fables. Each fable is woven into the next fable in the order given above to establish an intertwined correlation between tales.

Morals of Panchatantra

Panchatantra tales have a hidden agenda within them which is to imbibe strong moral and ethical messages to both its reader and the listener. The morals that they convey are to choose our friends wisely;

a sharp mind is the greatest strength; think before you act; do not build castles in the air, they will fall; unity is strength; a known demon is better than an unknown angel; a friend in need is a friend indeed; a mind that cannot judge on its own belives a lie to be a truth; it is better to use common sense over knowledge at times; think on your feet at the time of crisis; greed leads to disaster; when there is a quarrel between two friends the enemy benefits; always be solution-oriented; never to lie[9] – these are just a few to name, and many more can be added to the list.

It is pertinent to note here that these morals help a man to develop holistically. If we observe keenly we can find many similarities in the teaching of the Gita, Arthashastra, Vedas, Puranas, Smritis, etc, and the morals of Panchatantra. These tales preach dharma, virtue, integrity, righteousness, and many more values in the simplest of ways.

Panchatantra is one of the tools devised by our ancestors to educate us upon principles, values, ethics, and morals. In the era when there were no laws like we have now, the Panchatantra proved to be one of the easiest methods to affiliate the society with social norms, to sustain it on a noble path.

The great Greek philosopher and the Father of Political Science, Aristotle once argued that "morality is something we learn as we are born as amoral creatures", as men we have a natural desire for possession and hunger for power, we tend to establish a state where 'Matsya Nyaya' prevails i.e, 'Law of the Jungle' where the powerful prey on the weak, but teachings and preachings of dharma and niti help us to establish a 'Ram Rajya' where the powerful loot for and take care of the meek. The tales of Panchatantra are one of the ways to keep in check the oscillation of the society between anarchy and order.

Conclusion

Indian culture plays a very important role in inculcating ethical values. Indian values have always given prime importance to the right to happiness for all human beings.

Indian culture is a complex and intricate structure. The two most important tenets of Indian culture are human values and holism. Human values refer to moral, spiritual, and ethical values while Holism means oneness or unity. Indian culture is very rich and diverse and teaches us to be tolerant of others. Important values taught to us from time immemorial are ever relevant and unchanging are found in the form of scriptural texts, folk tales, the Epics, the Gitas, the Dhammapada, Jataka Tales, Panchatantra, etc.[10]

These basic morals and values are relevant even today. The tenets of our culture that were naturalistic, every man and woman had to follow to experience their life to its fullest extent. Even today we follow these norms and morals, few of them as a social obligation while some of them have been legalized by the lawmakers of our nation. The Principles of Natural Justice are nothing but a revised form of Natural Justice. Article 14, 19, and 21 which is also the golden triangle[11]of our Indian Constitution have drawn their inspiration from natural law.

The stories and tales of Panchtantra may play a very small role in our lives but their impact is huge. We all are well acquainted with the stories of Panchatantra and it is the morals of these stories that pave the path for us to understand the intricacies of much more complicated and intricates values in our life. These stories act like our baby steps to become a part of a sustainable society. Plato once said that a "man without ethics is a wild beast loosed upon this world", and the Panchatantra Tales helps us to rein this beastly behaviour of a man in gentle yet efficacious ways.

The tales of Panchatantra keep on breathing among us, people have come and gone but the morals of these stories have been etched in our hearts, and I can also assure you that they will keep on living. Teaching mankind the basics and basis of lifc so we can tread in this stream called life with ease and dignity.

CHAPTER TWO

RIGHT OF PRIVATE DEFENSE OF PROPERTY (SECTIONS 103-105 OF IPC, 1860)

Author: Roshni Agarwal, II year of B.A.,LL.B.(Hons.) from Amity Law School, Noida

Roshni Agarwal

Section 103: When right of private defense of property extends to causing death[i]

A person may cause death in safeguarding his own property or the property of someone else when there is a reason to apprehend that the person whose death is caused was about to commit or was attempting to commit one of the offenses mentioned in the said section as:

1. Robbery
2. House Breaking by night
3. Mischief by fire on any building, tent or vessel which is used as a human dwelling or as a place for the custody of property
4. Theft, mischief or house trespass under such circumstances when there is reasonable apprehension that death or grievous hurt would be the consequence if such right of private defense is not exercised[ii].

In the first three offences, death of a person can be caused who is committing or attempting to commit these offenses.

But, in case of the fourth clause, condition is attached which is that there should be reasonable apprehension of death or grievous hurt. Further, in case of theft, the said right cannot be exercised if the need for its exercising arises because of the intervention of the person who is exercising such right. Also, in case of trespass, such right is not available is case of an open land because Section 103 mentions about house trespass and not criminal trespass.

In case of Ismail[iii], the accused caused the death of a person who had trespassed into his courtyard in the middle of the night by striking him on the head three times with a club. Right of private defense of property under clause 4 of Section 103 granted by the court and the accused was not held liable because he did not know, in the middle of the night in the dark, that how dangerous was the person who had trespassed into his house, was armed or not. So, there was reasonable apprehension of death or grievous hurt.

Section 104: When such right extends to causing any harm other than death[iv]

This section justifies causing of any harm short of death in the exercise of the right of private defense of property if the offense committed or attempted to be committed is theft, mischief or criminal trespass[v]. In such case, the person in possession of property has right to defend against anyone trying to enter his property to prevent himself from getting dispossessed, maintain the possession and eject the accused. (Baljit Singh vs. State of UP)[vi]

Further, this right under section 104 to cause harm is available only if there is no time of having recourse to protection of public authorities. Eg: B enters A's farm and starts uprooting the crops. B has private defense to cause harm to B other than that causing death in order to prevent his sown crops from being destroyed.

Exception: This right lost when the trespasser enters the property and the trespass is accomplished successfully. Eg: B trespassed A's land and took its unlawful possession two years ago. Now, A does not have right of private defense against B. Now, he has to take recourse to the remedies available under the law to discharge B from his property and regain possession of it.

The Supreme Court in A.R. Yalve v. State of Maharashtra[vii] held that the right of private defense under sections 103 and 104 is not available in cases where the accused does have the right, title, interest or possession over the disputed land.

Section 105: Commencement and continuation of the right of private defense of property[viii]

The right of private defense of property commences when a reasonable apprehension of danger to the property commences. Thus, commencement of actual danger to the property is not necessary as this right is not a right of retaliation. So, one need not wait until the aggressor starts committing the offense but mere apprehension of it is sufficient in order to exercise this right.

1. Right of Private Defense of Property against Theft

Continues till or ends when:

(i) The offender has effected his retreat with the property i.e. has made his escape and left the property.

(ii) Assistance of public authorities is obtained

(iii) Property has been recovered.

2. Right of Private Defense of Property against Robbery

Continues as long as the offender causes or attempts to cause to any person death or hurt or wrongful restraint or as long as the fear of instant death or of instant hurt or instant personal restraint continues. The use of the word "instant" here is important[ix]. The right is available only as long as the fear is instant and not after the robbery has ended, the robber has left the property and one met him the other day.

3. Right of Private Defense of Property against Criminal Trespass or Mischief

Continues as long as the offender continues in the commission of the criminal trespass or mischief. In Hukam Singh[x], the accused (B) forcibly took two carts loaded with sugarcane through the field of A in which there were standing crops, in transporting them to the public passage running by the side of A's field. Till the time B is in the course of committing such forcible, intentional criminal trespass, A has this right against him. It does not matter that B cannot get out of the field without committing further criminal trespass.

4. Right of Private Defense of Property against House Breaking by Night

Continues as long as the house-trespass which has begun by such housebreaking continues.

In Rizan v. State of Chattisgarh[xi], the Supreme Court ruled that under Sections 102 and 105 of IPC, the right of private defense commences as soon as there arises reasonable apprehension of threat or attack on person or property, and continues till such reasonable apprehension continues to exist.

CHAPTER THREE

THE ROLE OF WTO IN DSU: AN ANALYSIS

Author: Aditi Agarwal, I year of LL.M. from Christ (Deemed To Be) University, Central Campus

Aditi Agarwal

INTRODUCTION

The core function of a trade dispute settlement mechanism in international commerce is to act as an effective custodian of the rules-based system. From the General Agreement on Tariffs and Trade (GATT) to the current day, the evolution of dispute settlement in international trade indicates an increasing significance to a system that is not dependent on power. The previous system was ineffective and lacked appropriate political control. The WTO system is praised as a breakthrough in international economic relations that goes beyond power. Despite this huge progress, the current system is still neutral in certain ways.

WTO dispute settlement features specific procedural norms, an appeals process, and back-up arbitration mechanisms to deal with non-implementation and the computation of trade sanctions in response to ongoing non-compliance, in comparison to most other international adjudication systems.For poor nations wanting to protect their trade rights and development objectives, the World Trade Organization (WTO) dispute settlement procedure might be crucial. The system has been critical in combating damaging subsidy programmes, reducing unjust anti-dumping charges, and guaranteeing that Least Developed Countries (LDCs) may pursue trade diversification policies to provide new employment and income possibilities.

There has been an upsurge in cross-border trade between nations over the years. With technological advancements resulting in a new global business paradigm, trade and governmental bodies such as the World Trade Organization (WTO) and Regional Arbitrations have stepped up efforts to end protectionism, establish liberalised cross-border trade, and eliminate the prevalence of beggar-thy-neighbour economic policies.

Developed nations are in a far better position than developing countries, and as a result, many underdeveloped countries do not consider using an international platform. This is mostly due to the exorbitant expense of involvement and the unpredictability of the advantages. In international law the term dispute means a specific disagreement relating to a question of rights or interests in which the parties proceed by the way of claims, counterclaims, denials and so on.[i] In another definition, dispute in international law is a situation when one entity of international law demands from another one specific action or behaviour and such a demand is based on the rules of international law binding for both parties and this other entity resists this action or behaviour.[ii]As a result, the term disagreement differs from conflict, which refers to a general state of animosity between the parties. The distinction is important, since opposite to the conflicts, disputes are not entirely undesirable and may have certain valuable characteristics such as an effect of law clarification.[iii]

In the context of the WTO Dispute Settlement system, the term dispute stands for a situation in which one WTO Member State adopts a trade policy or measure or takes some action, that one or more concerned WTO Members consider to be a breach of the WTO Agreements or a failure to meet obligations under such agreements.[iv]

Most importantly, WTO members have regularly employed the dispute settlement mechanism, which has successfully resolved disputes in the vast majority of instances with significant exceptions. Without a good understanding of the history of international trade through time, a complete and successful examination of the shaping forces of international commerce and the settlement of international trade disputes is impossible.

At the same time, the WTO must ensure that disputes are resolved quickly and that retaliation is replaced with alternative viable remedies. However, the Agreements, including the DSU, appear to contain significant flaws that might encourage a nation to break the WTO's trade regulations. The DSU's inability to offer an effective and timely response to such deviations significantly jeopardises the WTO's whole multilateral trade system. Despite the enthusiastic vows made by WTO members, the results of WTO Ministerial Meetings illustrate that multilateral trade negotiations may nevertheless end in gridlock and failure. An effective WTO dispute settlement system because it serves the public interest.

The 1994 signing of the World Trade organization (WTO) Agreement marked theinitiation of the most far-reaching and comprehensive international agreement on trade inthe history of the modern world[v]. The creation of an actual trade organization was amarked improvement over the WTO's predecessor, the 1994 GATT, Among the manyimprovements to the GATT, the WTO Agreement substantially changed the mechanismfor dispute settlement wheneverconflict arose between member states.[vi] This change, was initially hailed as a great improvement over the GATT dispute settlement provisions.[vii]

Unfortunately, the DSU has not been the comprehensive dispute settlement mechanism its framers had hoped to create.[viii]

<u>THE PROBLEM</u>

As a WTO member, a nation is obligated to participate in WTO discussions, which involve trade liberalisation. When a country conducts commerce with another country, disagreements are unavoidable, and countries must use the DSU in such circumstances. However, the Agreements, including the DSU, appear to contain various flaws that might encourage a nation to break from the WTO's trade standards. The current study aims to analyse the effects of the DSU's deficiencies and focuses on what the WTO should do to offer quick and appropriate remedies for unfair trade practises.

HISTORY OF DISPUTE SETTLEMENT SYSTEM

GATT DISPUTE SETTLEMENT

The mechanism by which GATT judged trade problems was first formalised in an appendix to the 1979 Understanding on Dispute Settlement, and it bears a lot of similarities with the DSU system. A case would begin with a request for consultations, just as it does now. A complainant would request a panel procedure if a mutually suitable solution to the disagreement could not be reached during negotiations. The twist in this scenario is that, under the GATT, a defendant might deny the complainant's request for a panel, a prospect that has long been viewed as one of the system's most blatant flaws[ix]. Interestingly, few defendants blocked requests for a panel.[x] Rather, they routinely obstructed the acceptance of panel recommendations, exploiting GATT's other well-known flaw.

The first of these gaps was addressed in 1989 with the Dispute Settlement Procedures Improvements, which gave complainants the right to a GATT panel. Defendants could no longer prevent or considerably delay a panel request, even while the potential of non-adoption loomed large. The EC recognised that the Improvements had removed the strategy of delay in the GATT-era Bananas instances, for example, and encouraged the panel not to go too hastily in hearing this intricate issue[xi]. In this approach, the Improvements provided a method for complainants to avoid the consultation stage's "power politics." Perhaps notsurprisingly, the Improvements were thus argued to have revitalized dispute settlement[xii], given GATT "teeth,"[xiii] and encouraged the paneling of disputes more generally.[xiv]

Despite its infamous flaws, the system was quite effective overall. However, in those cases that got to trial, 83 percent of the decisions favoured the plaintiff, but only 63 percent of the time, concessions were granted, indicating the system's inadequacy at the compliance stage[xv]. The early settlement was for 59 percent out of all concessions made, showing importance of this stage in the GATT process.

PRINCIPAL SHORTCOMINGS OF GATT DISPUTE SETTLEMENT SYSTEM

The growing volume and complexity of trade disputes between an expanding number of member nations has clearly put excessive strain on a system that was not meant to handle such economic, legal, and political demands[xvi]. These flaws were exposed in three high-profile examples of non-compliance during the GATT's last years. Nevertheless, it is important to realize that, given the alternative forms of international dispute settlement available, the GATT system must be recognized has having been a success.[xvii]Further, inspite of its short comings, the GATT dispute settlement system servedits purpose sufficiently well to form part of the foundations of the WTO Dispute Settlement Understanding..[xviii]The growing volume and complexity of trade disputes between an expanding number of member nations has clearly put excessive strain on a system that was not meant to handle such economic, legal, and political demands. These flaws were exposed in three high-profile examples of non-compliance during the GATT's last years.

- The relevant Articles were short and without explicit objectives and procedures, resolution was reliant on the formation of ad hoc methods
- Ambiguity about the function of consensus, which results in the 'blocking' of negative choices
- Due to the lack of a right to a panel and no firm time limitations on any component of the proceedings[xix], there were delays and ambiguity in the dispute resolution process.
- Delays in panel rulings, as well as partial non-compliance with them.

THE WTO DSU AND THE URUGUAYROUND NEGOTIATIONS

The WTO Dispute Settlement Understanding (DSU) replaced the GATT system on January 1, 1995, and is considered one of the Uruguay Round's most important achievements. Before the Uruguay Round discussions initiated, the GATT Contracting Parties were in agreement that the dispute settlement system needed to be overhauled. Negotiations shall include the development of adequate arrangements for overseeing and monitoring of the procedures that would facilitate compliance with adopted recommendations.[xx]This isn't to claim that there was unanimous agreement on how a new conflict resolution mechanism should be built. One of Canada's, the EU's, and Japan's main goals, as well as many other developing nations', was to limit the United States' use of unilateral action, which is allowed under federal law, the adoption of a rule-oriented approach (automaticity), a defined timeframe for dispute resolution, and agreement on the possibility for cross-retaliation were the main goals of the US. The

United States and other Members are constrained from acting unilaterally in many ways[xxi]. Members' national legislation must conform with their duties under the WTO, according to Article XVI.4 of the Agreement Establishing the WTO. Members are also required to follow the DSU's rules and procedures. The DSU incorporates the US objective of automaticity as a pivotale lement of the dispute settlement process.[xxii]Article 20 establishes a precise, and hence predictable, timeframe for the resolution of disputes. Article 22.3 addresses the limited possibilities for cross-retaliation between sectors in the event of non-compliance.

PROCEDURE FOLLOWED BY THE WTO's DSU TO SETTLEMENT TRADE DISPUTES

The WTO's distinctive contribution to the global economy is dispute settlement, which is the key pillar of the multilateral trade system. The rule-based system would be less successful if there was no way to resolve conflicts since the rules could not be enforced[xxiii]. The WTO method promotes the rule of law and improves the trade system's security and predictability. The system is based on clearly –defined rules, with timetables forcompleting a case.[xxiv] The goal of DSU is to resolve conflicts as quickly as possible, preferably through talks.

INDIA IN WTO'S DISPUTE SYSTEM REGIMEASONE OF THE LEADING DEVELOPING COUNTRIES

The Dispute Settlement Understanding (DSU) of the WTO is widely regarded asthe "backbone of the multilateral trading system".[xxv] The notion of "automaticity," "crossretaliation," rigorous timetables, and the ability to submit appeals before an appellate body were all established by the new DSU, ensuring that developing nations could play a more significant part in the dispute resolution system. The first several years of WTO dispute resolution were eye-opening. During this period, the DSU's efficacy was put to the test.During this time, there were a slew of complaints from developed countries and between developing and developed countries. India's experience with the WTO's negotiation process and dispute resolution mechanism paints a quite different image. During this time, India emerged as a powerful actor and a strong voice for developing countries in international negotiations. The changes happened at a time when India's trade share was still very in significant; India's merchandise trade was less than 1 percent and services trade was less than 2 percent.[xxvi] One area where India's involvement was noticeable was in dispute resolution. In that context, a look at India's human, institutional, and stakeholder capability can help us figure out how it dealt with some of the most pressing issues. India was well aware of the ramifications of entering a multilateral trade agreement like the WTO.

Immediately after joining the WTO, India had to face challenges to its patent mail-box system from the U.S. and the EC.[xxvii]According to TRIPS Agreement if a member under Article 70 does not provide patent protection for pharmaceutical and agricultural chemical products as of the TRIPS Agreement's entry into force date, that Member must set up a system for filing patent applications for those products (known as "mail-box" filing). The goal of the mail box filing was to provide a legal foundation for determining filing and priority dates that would be utilized when these applications were subsequently assessed. In the lack of domestic law, India's use of "administrative instructions" does not offer a strong legal foundation for assuring conformity with the TRIPS Agreement, according to the Appellate Body. India's loss in these battles sparked a flurry of arguments in India, as well as a surge in interest in IPR issues.

As a respondent, India was challenged by the US for levying "additional duties" and "extra additional duties" on wine, spirits, and other agricultural and manufactured products, which the US claimed were in violation of WTO commitments, specifically Article II:1(a) and (b), as well as Article III:2 of the GATT. The panel found in India's favour, but the Appellate Body overturned the panel's decision. The disputed Additional Customs Duty was implemented to counterbalance the impact of state-level excise taxes on locally made goods. The tariff was set at the state's highest level of taxes. It was difficult to remove the import charge without also eliminating the excise duty on domestically produced wine and spirits.

CONCLUSION

The World Trade Organization's (WTO) dispute settlement mechanism appears to be an inextricable aspect of international economic law, and it's impossible to imagine the multilateral trading system without it. After all, the WTO's dispute resolution mechanism is one of the organization's success stories. There are, of course, objections and several ideas in the framework of DSU reform. However, no government is now advocating for the WTO dispute settlement system to be abolished. Indeed, many reform ideas ask for more efficient and effective conflict resolution. Modifications may be on the way, but the future of WTO dispute settlement is unquestionably secure.

States are prepared to sell a portion of their sovereignty for the benefits of coordinated efforts and international governance in the current era of globalization. Deep integration follows shallow integration, which includes everything from consultation to coordination and harmonization to coordination. States must create new means to resolve their issues on the international stage in such a world. The DSU will take another big stride toward strengthening the rule of law in international relations with an upgraded and reformed institutional compliance framework.

CHAPTER FOUR

COHABITATION FROM THE EYES OF THE LAW

Author: Sahil Gupta, II year of B.A.,LL.B.(Hons.) from Amity Law School, Noida (Amity University U.P)

Introduction

In India, Law and morality have always been related, either together or in contrast. On one side, Law provides us with rules and regulations for a specific community to be followed, while morals provide us with knowledge of right and wrong for society. History has witnessed that morals are the basis of law but with the changing society, laws have also played a significant role in establishing morals for a society. Like in the case of the Sati Act, earlier the sacrifice was morally correct in society but after the ban of the Sati act by Lord Bentinck, now the act is no more morally correct. Likewise, every generation, society, the community has its own myths and morals. The sources for these myths and man-made created morals are always unknown, but questioning them is still a chance of bearing risks. One such myth which has developed over a period of time is the Live-in relationship, known as Cohabitation in western countries like Australia, Canada, etc. The term live-in refers to living together of a couple without marrying but living a life like a married couple i.e., sharing intimate, emotional relationships with each other without fulfilling formalities of a valid marriage.

As law influence, morals of a society, giving legal status to the live-in relationship will help cohabitees to follow it with much ease. After the enactment of the Domestic Violence Act, 2005, everyone had a mindset that now Indian Legal System has accepted live-in relationships as "live-in" and "relationship in the nature of marriage" come from the same root. Likewise, Section-125 of Cr. P.C and Section-114 of the Indian Evidence Act,1872 also provide protection to the cohabitees. Earlier, the live-in relationship was restricted between a male and female, but with the changing times and after enactment of new laws for homosexual personalities, the band of live-in has broadened to homosexuals also. The concept of Live-in was enough for a hype situation in society but the addition of homosexuality added fuel to the fire Thought about live-in relationships, seems fantasizing to the youth and ill-practice to their parents. Due to generation gaps, old school romance minds, and many other reasons, many societies are unable to accept cohabitation to date. Through the virtue of this article, the phenomenon of cohabitation can be analysed and be understood by an individual.

This article talks about the legal status of live-in in India, comparison of the legal status of cohabitation with other countries like Scotland, France, Sweden, Australia, Russia, and more. Comparison of cohabitation with marriage, pros, and cons of cohabitation, reasons to why society is accepting live-in relationships. Also, a few cases along with their respective judgments are discussed.

Reasons for increase in Live-in relationships

In India, marriage is considered to be the most sacred and the only pure bond between a couple. The bond of marriage is always related to religion, law, and many social involvements. After the marriage, both the husband and wife are burdened with a lot of obligations and responsibilities towards each other as well as their respective families. In some cases, a woman is even not allowed to complete her higher studies whereas the male due to the responsibilities on him is unable to complete his studies after marriage. And in the case of divorce, many heartbreaks, many social stigmas are faced, many social, economic as well as mental consequences are faced by husband and wife. In a marriage, the wife is given the role to serve her husband whereas the husband is allotted a role to fulfil all economic needs of his wife.

Live-in is a concept, presenting western culture, i.e., to live in a way one wants with whom he/she wants, without any restrictions. With the emerging times, live-in has gained a lot of recognition all over the world, and now people are accepting it, exploring it due to the kind of flexibility it provides. Live-in is a secular concept, as it sees no religion, no caste, and no equalities on any basis including gender as well. In a live-in relationship, both the partners are independent and free from all liabilities that exist in married life. Both the partners can grow together, and learn together, treating each other equally. Also, in a live-in relationship divorce is not needed, thus socially, mentally, and economically safe from being ruined.

Earlier, there was no legislation for live-in but after the interpretation of some laws in case judgments by several courts, now live-in is legal. Women in a live-in relationship feel protected by the law, their children get maintenance from their father up to certain age and thus, the law has accepted the culture of live-in in India. In the recent case of Ajay Bhardwaj Vs. Jyotsna, Jyotsna was granted maintenance of twenty thousand rupees each month to her and ten thousand each month to both children each by the court from her live-in partner i.e., Ajay.

Laws for Live-in Relationship in India

Having deep roots in the ethics and morals of a society, it was very difficult for India to accept the live-in relationships, but to cope up with today's modern as well as western culture, India has also given live-in relationships, a green signal. Though there is still no particular law, no rights, no legal definition, or no obligations given to a live-in couple are prescribed under the constitution. But Courts through various case judgments have clarified, the legal status of live-in. Courts interpret and amend the legislation in order to prevent mishappening arising from live-in. Following are the legislations, used by courts to deal with cases of live-in:

Domestic Violence Act, 2005

Section-2(f) of the Domestic Violence Act, 2005 states definition for "domestic relationship". In the Indian history of law, this is the first legislation for females, with respect to the live-in relationship. Though live-in is not clearly mentioned in the Act, a hint for the same is given. It is left for courts to interpret the meaning of "relationship in the nature of marriage". As live-in and nature of marriage share common boundaries, thus courts assume protection of women in live-in under this act.

Criminal Procedure Code

On 24 November 2000, the Malimath Committee, i.e., the committee on reforms of the Criminal Justice System was formed by the Government of India to give a new structure to Criminal Justice System with all the necessary changes required. In 2003, the formed committee submitted its report and several recommendations were reported. In part-IV of the report, under the head of offenses against women, one of the suggestions was to amend Section-125 of CR.P.C, so as to expand the definition of a wife, i.e., the definition of the wife should include a woman who was living with a man as his wife for a reasonably long period, during the subsistence of the first marriage.Earlier, a woman in second marriage was not entitled to claim maintenance as she was not given the legal status of wife. In order to prevent the man to take advantage of this legal fact, the committee suggested amending section-125.

Indian Evidence Act, 1872

Section-114 of the Indian Evidence Act, 1872 states that a court can assume the existence of any facts which it thinks likely to happen, regard being had to the common course of natural events, human conduct, and public & private business, in their reference to the facts of the actual case.Therefore, a man and a woman living together for a very long time like a couple are assumed by courts to be married.

Landmark Judgements in Indian Courts

Case of Badri Prasad Vs Dy. Director of Consolidation was the first case in the Supreme Court to be dealt with the recognition of the live-in relationship. In this case, a 50-year-old live-in relationship was challenged legally but the court held that if a couple is asked to prove their relationship after completing 50 years together, then it will be possible for a few couples only. Thus, the court declared their relationship legally valid.

In the landmark case of Khushboo vs Kanniammal&Anr, Khushboo was an actress against whom 23 criminal complaints were filed for offenses under Sections 499, 500, and 505 of the IPC, 1860. Once, in an interview, she had talked about pre-marital sex and unwanted pregnancies, after the publication of this interview in India Today and DhinaThanti, she was exposed to great criticism. In the Court hearings, Court stated the examples for Radha & Krishna in support of her and also considered that how can it be illegal, when both the partners are adults and doing all sexual activities with the consent of both. Therefore, the court held it as not illegal.

In another landmark case of Indra Sarma Vs. V.K.V.Sarma, Indra, and V.K.V used to work in the same company and after some time, she left the company and started living together, although Indra was unmarried he had a wife with two children, but still, they continued to live together. He forced him, multiple times for abortion, also he used to take money from her at times. After some time, when she reached the court for her right in his property, Supreme Court stated that although she was aware of the fact about his married life, still she continued to live with him, which amounts to no relief to her under prescribed legislation also. But Supreme Court in order to protect partners in a live-in relationship against ill-practices felt the need to modify Section-2(f) in Pwdva,2005. After modification definition of domestic relationships also includes jobless, illiterate partners with their children born out of a live-in relationship. Supreme Court has also requested Parliament to enact new legislation for the same.

In the case of Alok Kumar Vs State, the complainant was in a live-in relationship with him, and he used to keep her promising that after his divorce with the first wife having a child also, he will marry her. Both Alok and Complainant used to have intimate relationships in London as well as in Delhi. One day when she caught Alok holding hands with another girl at the IGI Airport, she tried to talk to him but he beats her and ran. On registering FIR, she informed all other incidents too but when the matter came in the Delhi High Court, it held that "live-in is a walk-in & walk-out relationship with no legal restrictions attached. People who want to avoid such mishappenings should bind with the partner in a bond of marriage. In a live-in relationship, one cannot complain about immorality."

In Payal Sharma v. Nari Niketan, Payal Sharma was a 21-year-old girl, who was living with a man. The case was about the legality of the same. The Allahabad High Court held that "a man & a woman, even without getting married, can live together if they wish to. This may be regarded as immoral by society and to society, but it is not illegal from a legal point of view. There is a difference between law and morality."

Legal Status given to a child

According to the Hindu Succession Act, 1956 a legitimate child has the right to joint family property, but an illegitimate child could only inherit property from his mother's side but not from his father. In India, the legitimacy of a child and the inheritance of property have always been related but the courts have cleared through its judgments that a child born out of a live-in relationship has the right to property when born after a certain time period of the relationship.

In the landmark case of Vidyadhari Vs Sukhrana Bai, Sukhrana Bai was the first wife of Sheetaldeen and Vidyadhari was second. After the death of Sheetaldeen, Vidyadhari fought for her and her children's rights in the property of Sheetaldeen. In this case, the court held that as Sukhrana Bai was the first and legally wedded wife, therefore she has the right to the property of her husband. The court also considered that though, during the subsistence of the first marriage, the second marriage is void but the child born out of the second marriage has the right to property of their father. Thus, the property was divided among four children of Vidyadhari and Sukhrana Bai.

In some cases, courts have granted rights to the child, some have contradictory comments. While criticizing the judgment of the landmark case of Bharat Mata Vs Union of India, Justice Ganguli pointed out that in Section-16(3) of the Hindu Marriage Act, 1955 only the "property" word is mentioned, no specification i.e., ancestral or self-acquired property is done.

According to Section-21 of the Hindu Adoption Act, 1956 a son either legitimate or illegitimate till the age of eighteen years and a daughter until not married are dependent on their father and thus, they have the right to maintenance from the father or estate of their deceased father. Denial of maintenance to a child born out of a live-in relationship can be challenged under Article-21 of the Indian Constitution, 1949. Unequal treatment to the children born out of live-in can be treated as a violation of Article-14 of the Indian Constitution, 1949.

In Dimple Gupta Vs Rajiv Gupta, Dimple Gupta has filed an application through her mother against Rajiv Gupta seeking maintenance at Rs 500 per month from her father as she was born out of the live-in relationship between her father and her mother NarainDassi. In this case, Narain become pregnant when she was in her tenth class, on reaching the hospital for abortion both of them were informed that abortion can't be done as pregnancy is at an advanced stage. Thus, Dimple was an illegitimate child of Rajiv Gupta but the court held that Rajiv is responsible for paying maintenance every month. Through the virtue of justice, in this case, the court had stated that a child born out of a live-in relationship is legitimate and has the same rights as in the case of children from a valid marriage.

Child Custody at the time of termination of the relationship plays a crucial role in the life of a child as it can have diverse impacts on the life of him/her. There is no specified law for child custody in case of live-in but to resolve problems related to child custody, Courts have referred to Section-13 of Hindu Minority and Guardianship Act, 1956 & Guardian and Wards Act, 1890 which states that the welfare of the child should be given utmost priority. Also, a psychologist is appointed in order to understand his/her needs and desires for parents. HIZANAT in the Muslim Law states that all the rights and custody will be given to the mother and it cannot be denied until something contradictory is proved.

Country wise Analysis

Countries like Switzerland, Japan, Germany do not have laws for co-habitation whereas couples co-habiting are not punished either.

Australia

In Australia, a Live-in relationship is known as the de-facto relationship as defined under section-4AA of the Family Law Act, 1975. The Federal Circuit Courts deal with the issues of live-in relationships related to children in the same way as of married couples. From 01 March 2009, all the financial disputes related to the de-facto relationships are also solved at the Family Courts, but in order to solve disputes in front of the Court, some conditions should be fulfilled, like case to be filed within two years of breakdown, presence of a child, have a geographical connection to the participating jurisdiction, the relationship broke down after 01 March 2009.

Russia

Russia follows the Civil Law Tradition, derived from the Roman Law. Common Law and Doctrine are not the sources of law in Russia. Russia recognizes marriage only if it is registered in the Civil Acts Registered Office. None of the situations of cohabitation (i.e., duration of the relationship, child involved in a relationship, or any other circumstances) makes it legal. According to the Russian Laws, there are no agreements for the expense's division and property ownership, or assets distribution if one partner dies or leaves the relationship.

Scotland

In Scotland, rights are provided to all co-habitant couples but the rights are less than rights given to married couples. The rights are mentioned under the Family Law (Scotland) Act, 2006, which is applied to both same-sex as well as opposite sex couples. There are many rights given to the cohabitant couples, few amongst them are: equal share of household goods, money, property bought during the time-period of live-in, one can ask the court for financial provision at the time of separation, also one can ask for money/property of his/her partner, if the partner dies without writing his will, and one can apply court for domestic interdict also.

France

In France, earlier the law does not provide any obligation to the co-habiting couple but also does not provide any protection to the couples under the law. The cohabitation agreement depends on the will of the co-habitant couples, but it does not enforce obligations of ownership of property on them, i.e., the property is bought solely by one individual, then it belongs to him/her, but if bought by both, then both owns that property. Now, France Government has given legal status to unmarried couples, including homosexual couples also. The law has provided co-habitants with many different new laws such as they can help their foreign partners to enter the country & each partner will become liable for each other's debts, also the co-habitant couples can get benefits of filing a joint tax return after three years of registering their relation.

Canada

In Canada, a couple will be considered to be co-habiting only after successful completion of one year, they may live apart while maintaining the relationship. Co-habitation ends at the death of one partner or on the will of at least one partner. A co-habiting relationship cannot be established with more than one person at a time period, conjugal relationships are not allowed and of course, both the partners should not be minors. Like many other countries, Canada has also provided co-habiting couples with several different provisions like couples having children in the relationship, provisions for divorce including equal division of assets, debts. Unlike other countries, in Canada, no distinction is made in the eyes of law between married and cohabiting couples.

Pros and Cons of Live-in relationship

As every coin has two sides, likewise live-in has its own merits and demerits, which are equally important. The pros and cons of a live-in relationship are as follows:

Every individual has framed a demeanour, conduct as well as a character for their partner. But a reality check comes after living together with him/her. That's why nowadays live-in relationship is increasing. It serves as a test before marriage and helps the individuals to select a life partner after testing all compatibilities, like this life after marriage is also lived and foreseen by the partners. Live-in helps an individual to learn how to do household chores, how to manage them within their monthly budgets along with the savings for the future. It gives a realistic approach to learning and practicing freedom but with having responsibilities of house and themselves. On living together under the same roof as a married couple, both the partners will get to know about their as well as their partner's sexual desires. They will learn about each other's urges and their body needs along with their capacities. Some divorces are due to the sexual problems of partners, so these divorces will also be reduced.

Some cohabiting couples have deep bonding than those who straightforwardly got married because while live-in, both partners tend to appreciate each other's effort, and mutual respect is there whereas, in a marriage, efforts are taken for granted. Living together for the purpose of knowing each other, forces an individual to find good in their partners and love them with their worst also. So, therefore the relationship is deepened and enriched in live-in. Both the partners in a live-in relationship are financially independent of each other, they can spend for their own purpose on their own, they don't have to seek permission from the other. Also, some people tend to save money by joining households such as mortgages, utilities, house maintenances, and other household chores, in all these factors cost is reduced to half. Thus, it provides financial freedom to both the partners in live-in. At the time of the breakup, the partners have to face very few legal consequences in comparison to divorce after marriage. Partners are not obligated to give any property to others at the time of separation. Thus, in live-in a lot of ease is given to both the partners from the legal point of view.

In cohabitation there are very few restrictions, from society as well as from family, therefore, uncertainty in the relationship is high. The couples want to have a perfect relation including a perfect state of emotional as well as sexual desires, and due to non-fulfillment of such high ambitious imaginations, mostly breakups happen. On living together, couples save many sorts of money like house rent, household chores payment, etc., as all of these are halved, but there are many other benefits which they lose in comparison to a married couple, i.e., cohabiting couples have to pay an estate tax, cohabiting couples on gifting something have to face many consequences, health insurance rates are higher than a married couple, etc. In this twenty-first century, most societies still have many conflicting views for co-habitation. It is still considered a taboo in societies. The one who decides to co-habit has to face many social consequences like social boycott, houses on rent are not given to a co-habiting couple, etc. In co-habitation, both the partners are independent, they are testing before marriage, thus both are free and no restrictions lie there. There is less monogamy while in a cohabitation relationship. In a cohabitation, one has to ensure that his/her estate goes to his partner because if no specifications are made then all the property will be given to the next kin instead of the partner. Specifications to be made are that will to be written, with making partner as a primary beneficiary.

Conclusion

Live-in is neither a bad concept nor a good one. It is upon an individual, how he/she understands it. Every culture has its own merits and demerits, it's upon individuals of a society, how they perceive it. Morals and ethics are terms that are set by a society, by generations, these morals need to be modified in order to maintain pace with modern times. In India, there are no specific laws for live-in but some legislations are interpreted to make the concept of live-in legal. The legislations considered appropriate to be read in live-in related cases involve- Section-2(f) of the Domestic Violence Act, Section-125 of CR.P.C, Section114 of the Indian Evidence Act, Section-21 of the Hindu Adoption Act, and many others. There are many cases in which court have proved that live-in relationship is legal in India. For example, in the case of Badri Prasad Vs Dy. Director of Consolidation, the court held that the relationship was valid.

Globally also, live-in is legalized. In countries like Switzerland, Japan, Germany no laws are laid down for cohabitation but live-in is also not illegal either. In many countries like France, Canada, Australia, etc., cohabitees are protected under the law. All over the globe, people are accepting and welcoming this new culture of living together. Marriage is a social institution but still, many crimes occur after marriage also like marital rape, domestic violence, and many more, so we cannot blame marriage for those crimes, likewise live-in cannot be pre-assumed as a deviance factor in society. It's the need of a society, that learns more about live-in and then makes a rational decision. As change is the only constant thing in this world, thus society needs to think and work upon the same

Author Bio

his article is written by Sahil Gupta, He is a second-year law student pursuing B.A.LLB HONS course from the Amity Law School, Noida. He has contributed significantly by editing and writing a chapter for the book, "The Paradox of the Tribal Culture". Also, his news briefs were published in December 2020, News bulletin of Lexstructor Journal. Not achieved so much, but he has the zeal to learn and achieve a lot.

CHAPTER FIVE

PROTECTION OF DISABLED PEOPLE IN ARMED CONFLICT

Author: Satwik Sengupta, V year of B.A.,LL.B.(Hons.) from Amity Law School, Delhi (GGSIPU)

Introduction

The United Nations Security Council unanimously adopted resolution 2475(2019), which talks about the protection of disabled people in the situation of armed conflicts. This resolution was adopted on 20th June, 2019 in the 8556th meeting of the United Nations Security Council. On this day, the council called upon all its 15 members to decide unanimously on the vital matter at hand and to request all parties indulging in the practices of armed conflict on the international level to allow and facilitate timely, indiscriminatory and unrestricted access to humanitarian resolutions to all people in need of assistance in case of any significant problem arising out of such conflicts. and to prevent any sort of abuse or violence against civilians in scenarios pertaining to armed conflict. This meeting further encouraged all the present member states to ensure that any person with disability should have equal provisions of enjoyment of basic services like health care, sanitation, education, transportation and information and communication technology (ICT). The council also urged the present member states to enable meaningful representation and participation of persons with disabilities in various important and valuable organisations on the international pedestal.

Background

The inception of such ground breaking resolution came with the Convention on the Rights of Person with Disabilities (CRPD). This convention is considered as a touchstone in the aspect of giving equal rights and treatment to persons with disabilities. It was stated by the World Health Organisation (WHO) that around 15% of the world population (which is roughly 1 billion people) have or suffer from some form of disability varying merely on the basis of the magnitude of it. Out of such population, an approximate of 9.7 million people have been displaced due to armed conflict on the international sphere by the states and any other form of humanitarian violation. The Convention on the Rights of Person with Disabilities (CRPD) resulted in the formulation of various legislations in regard to the subject at hand and it was joined by 161 states. The most vital Article of such convention is Article 11 which states that "take, in accordance with their obligations under international law, including international humanitarian law and international human rights law, all necessary measures to ensure the protection and safety of persons with disabilities in situations of risk, including situations of armed conflict, humanitarian emergencies and the occurrence of natural disasters." The resolution 2475(2019) urged all the member party states to comply with all the regulations formed due to the CRPD and therefore ensure that the safety and security of the people during these scenarios.

Differing Opinions

The meeting regarding the discussion and acceptance of the resolution lasted for about 20 minutes, commencing from 9:31a.m. To 9:53a.m,implying that there was not much discussion and debate regarding the acceptance of the resolution. However, there were few delegates who highlighted some aspects of the resolution which in their opinion was flawed. One such delegate was Gennady V. Kuzmin, representing the Russian Federation. He noted that the protection of the disabled persons suggested by the resolution at hand should not come at the cost of the other people of the society. He stressed on the point that there should be a level of equality when considering the situation of protection of all people in the scenario of armed conflict. The suggestion made by the delegate was that the United Nations should not invent any new international legal concepts which would resulting in devising new categories of individuals who should require specific protection under the provisions of international humanitarian law and have an obligatory effect on the states.Striking the same chord, Yao Shaojun, a delegate representing the People's Republic of China stated that the issue of protection of person with disabilities should be dealt with according to the prevalent Council resolutions which talk about the protection of civilians and he also added thatthis responsibility was something which needed to be shouldered by all the states and the United Nations should play a complimentary role in it.[4]

Issues Raised

The contentions made by the Delegates can be summarised as:

1. No new international legislations for specific tasks: Out of the many points put forth by the delegate representing the Russian Federation, the most basic and main point was that there should not be any new legislation on the international front which would maybe lead to not following of the other prevalent regulations present within the United Nations. This till an extent is a valid point because if the states focus on the new legislation formulated then tit may cause some sort of violation or negligence towards other provisions of the same nature. The counsel Kuzmin, linked this point with the issue regarding the aspect of equality in protecting people from situations regarding armed conflict. His basic point of contention was that due to these legislations which enable special provisions for disabled persons, it may prove to be a hindrance for the general population of people who are also equally subject to the harshness caused due to these acts of armed conflicts. The Counsel was of the opinion that this legislation should not be such which shall create a kind of reservation for the targeted category of people. According to the delegate, there should not be a requirement of a separate legislation for tackling this problem as the United Nations already has many provisions regarding the subject matter which this legislation or resolution talks about.

2. Obligatory effect: According to the 'partly dissenting' delegate, the wordings of the resolution were ambiguous in pointing out the fact that whether this resolution was obligatory in nature and implies that every participant state shall follow that resolution mandatorily or it was of such nature that if a state wishes to follow the resolution it may implying a degree of discretion on the party states. Although Article 25 of the U.N Charter imposes an obligation upon the member states of the United Nation to "accept and carry out the decisions of the Security Council ..."there is no clear consensus regarding the required language that needs to be used to express the intention of the United Nations to ascertain a factor of obligation upon the member states.

The International Court of Justice gave an advisory opinion on the matter related to the obligatory nature of resolutions under Article 25 of the United Nations Charter in its 1971 Namibia Advisory Opinion. The

1971 Namibia Advisory Opinion was the result of the approach made by the Security Council to the International Court of Justice regarding the situation wherein there was continued presence of South Africa in the internal matters of Namibia. The International Court of Justice then upholding the views of the Security Council advised the South African authorities to curtail their continued presence in Namibia as the Security Council had passed an obligatory order regarding the same. However, it was challenged during the proceedings by the South African Authorities that there was no clear indication that such order was obligatory or not. That is when, in their relevant statement the International Court of Justice put forth their opinion that "The language of a resolution of the Security Council should be carefully analysed before a conclusion can be made as to its binding effect. In view of the nature of the powers under Article 25, the question whether they have been in fact exercised is to be determined in each case, having regard to the terms of the resolution to be interpreted, the discussions leading to it, the Charter provisions invoked and, in general, all circumstances that might assist in determining the legal consequences of the resolution of the Security Council."

Moreover, the former legal advisor for the United States Department Of State, John Bellinger has articulated that there has been a consensus amongst many international lawyers that there are three major factors which determines if a resolution is to be considered binding or not and those are:

1. That the legislation deals with counteracting any sort of threat to international peace and security
2. If the legislation mentions that the United Nations is acting under Chapter VII of the UN charter
3. Usage of the word 'Decides' in any operative paragraph which intends to be binding

On the contrary, the resolution 2475 uses words like "requests", or "suggests" clearly implying that the resolution is not binding but act like a set of guidelines (similar in nature to the Directive Principles of State Policy present in the Indian Constitution).

Conclusion

In conclusion, I would like to shed light on the fact that the basic principle feature of the resolution is to curtail the humanitarian and social abuse faced by the Disabled people and even though the Legislation is not binding upon the member states it has to be a primary focus of all the member countries to follow the guidelines given under such legislation as it promotes equality and hopes to curtail acts of unnecessary violence.

CHAPTER SIX

DOMESTIC VIOLENCE AGAINST MEN; THE SILENT CRISIS

Author: Atul Ratna, Research scholar from T.N.B Law college Bhgalpur

Co-author: Sumit Kumar Mishra, Research scholar from T.N.B Law college Bhgalpur

Co-author: Dr. Dhiraj Kumar Mishra, Asst. professor (LAW) from T.N.B Law college Bhgalpur

Atul Ratna

"The more that we choose not to talk about domestic violence, the more we shy away from the issue, the more we lose."

-Russell Wilson

No one can deny the fact that domestic violence is a grave issue in India as well world-wide. It can be defined as the violence by one spouse to another in the household. In our Indian society, we generally believe that certain sex is dominant over the passive one. The general thought of the patriarchal culture is that male members are much more dominant over the female and are positioned superior to the others.

But in the today's scenario, the circumstances is quite different than the previous one. Not only the females but male are also subject to the domestic violence. They are also being physically, mentally, emotionally as well as sexually abused by the females in various cases.

In simple words, domestic violence against man can be demarcated as a kind of hateful violence done against the man by the woman. And the pity reality is that the victim feels so embarrassed to reveal it out before the public. In India, there is no any law to protect the violence and the abuse committed against the man. We are far much behind in that step. Here, usually it is believed that the women are fragile and recurrent subject to the violence committed by man which are most of the time true. However, there are also infrequent but true situation is that man are also subject to the domestic violence by the women. The recent flow of feminism as well as the women empowerment in the name of fight against the patriarchal society, anenormous group of victims are being unnoticed.

The lack of awareness among the people regarding this issue is a matter of great concern. People as well as the patriarchal society makes fun of those men who come out of the box with their glitches. It is the general notion of the society that the man who comes out and grumble regarding the issue have lost their "masculinity". They are being mocked and these matters are hardly believed by anybody in the society. There are overabundance of cases where the women have falsely alleged her husband of mental and physical abuse to harass and make huge amount of money. In the leading case of Mr Markapuram Siva Rao and others vs. state of Andhra Pradesh[i], the honourable court found that the case was totally untrue and was made to harass the husband and their family to make a huge amount of money. The court quashed the proceeding and held it as abuse of the process of the court. Furthermore, in the case of Binod kumar singh vs. state of Jharkhand and others[ii], it was found that the women filed false case against the husband under section 498(a) of the IPC to mentally harass and to have huge amount of money from the latter.

From all over India, 98% of the respondents had suffered domestic violence more than once in their lives. The study enclosed Indian husbands from various socioeconomic strata, but the bulk of the respondents, according to the researchers, came from the upper middle class and the middle class[iii].

The first and foremost pace to resolve these kind of matters is to make the laws to shield the rights of the man and tackle the cases of false allegations against the victim. The laws must be made in such a way that help the victims to get freedom from their abusers and also reinstate the physical, mental and emotional health of the victims. The legislative makers must also enshrine the concept of economic compensation in cases of false and fake domestic violence cases. The rehabilitation homes must also be established so that the victim can come out of trauma of violence. The gender prejudiced law sometimes gives major loopholes to the women and they catch such loopholes to file fake cases against the man to harass them mentally. So, these kind of issues must also be seen so that action can be taken properly.

The state as well as the centre shall have to work together to acknowledge and recognise the problem and get to the solution. The basic natural right of victim i.e. right to be heard must be respected and they must be allow to present their grievances before the other. The media which is the fourthpillar shall also have to play vital roles in these issues. They shall have to make aware to the general people regarding the contemporaneousproblems of the society which is being occurred.

Apart from them the law schools must also conduct seminar and workshop to make the people aware since the law schools are the factory of budding lawyers and law makers.

Despite of modern laws and principles of equity and justice, the victims are unable to stand up against their grievances and to claim relief against such kind of abuse. The society need to understand the elementary thing that domestic violence is a heinouscrime in the society by one spouse to other and one thing must be kept clear in the mind that it is gender neutral. The victim can be any gender be it male or female. It is the silence of the society that is sprinkling the current problem and harnessing the victim to come out and fight for their rights.

Author's Bio

The author has completed his B.A.LL.B(H) as well as LL.M from Central university of south bihar. He is currently pursuing Ph.D from T.N.B Law college, Bhagalpur.

CHAPTER SEVEN

A CRITICAL STUDY OF DOMESTIC VIOLENCE

Author: Sheikh Aman Rana, Pursuing LL.M. from Chanakya National Law University

Sheikh Aman Rana

INTRODUCTION

"Of all the evils for which man has made himself responsible, none is so degrading, so shocking or so brutal as his abuse of the better half of humanity; the female sex." Mahatma Gandhi, the Father of Nation.

From the times since immemorial, men and women have worked and contributed together in the sustenance and development of their families and later to the generations to come. In the early Vedic period, women were treated equally in every sphere of society. They were given a prestigious position in society. There is a Shloka in Sanskrit that cross-examines the above statements which "yatra naarya stupuuj yanter amante ta trade vataahya traitaa stunapuuj yantesar vaastatraa phalaah kriyaa" which means, where a woman is respected, the place becomes God's abode, by God's abode, it means, divine qualities, good deeds, peace, and harmony. It was a wonderful period for Women. However, in the following periods, there were various setbacks to this situation. There is an extract from the Ramcharitmanas which states that 'Dhol, Gauwnaar, Shudra, Pashuour Nari; SakalTadan ka Adhikari' [drums, uncivilized illiterates, lower castes, animals and women are all fit to be beaten] is evidenceof women's declining status in the society. Even in the later periods like the Medieval periods, the condition of women and their rights was still degrading. There were restrictions put on the rights and privileges of women and the conditions of women were only further deteriorating. British periods saw the mixed scenarios of women's status where one hand there were cases of the Sati System, Child marriage, female infanticide arose[1], on the other hand, various reformers played a crucial part in curbing such menaces against women. The womenwere always looked down as an inferior gender where her roles and duties are fixed by society even before she is born.

In Contemporary India, the Constitution provides for equal opportunity and rights of all in society. The Preamble of the Constitution provides to all citizens equal opportunity and equality of status. Article 14 of the Constitution guarantees equality before the law to all citizens within the land of India[2]. Article 15[3]forbids discrimination on the basis of religion, race, caste, sex, and place of birth, or any of them. Article 51-A (e) in Part IV-A provides a fundamental duty that it is the duty of every citizen to renounce practices derogatory to the dignity of women. Even after so many provisions for the betterment of the status of women, the women in India have been the victims of different forms of violence.

All these Laws and statutes are nothing more than a mirage for the women who have to face violence within the four walls of the house which is supposed to be the safest place in the whole world for them. Such abuse or violence is called domestic violence either by the intimate partner or the other family members. It is an extreme form of abuse as it is committed by the institution which is supposed to be a place of love, affection, warmth, care, and solidarity, and utmost care is expected from it i.e.Family. This is the reason why domestic violence is more than just violence as it causes a mental trauma and psychological effect upon the person affected. This violence can take the forms of physical assault, financial abuse, sexual abuse, and psychological abuse.

CONCEPT OF DOMESTIC VIOLENCE

Domestic Violence can be defined as a pattern of behavior in which one person is trying to control another person by way of coercion, threat, violent behavior, harassment including sexual violence in a domestic setting such as in marriage or cohabitation. Domestic violence occurs in various forms such as emotional, physical, sexual, etc.

The Protection of Women from Domestic Violence Act 2005[4] provides a broad definition of domestic violence. Section 37 defines domestic violence includes any act or conduct or omission, or commission of respondent who harms or injures, or endangers the health, safety, life, limb, or well-being, whether mental or physical of the aggrieved person or tends to do so

It includes:

1. Physical abuse means any act which causes bodily pain, harm, or danger to life, limb, or health and includes assault, criminal intimidation, and criminal force.
2. Sexual abuse means any act of sexual nature which violates the dignity of a human being.
3. Verbal and emotional abuse insults, ridicule, humiliation, name-calling, and specially for not having a male child and repeated threats of physical pain to any person in whom the aggrieved person is interested.
4. Economic abuse includes deprivation of all or any economic or financial resources to which aggrieved person is entitled under any law or custom or disposal of household effects or prohibition or restriction to continued access to resources or facilities to which aggrieved person is entitled.

Domestic legal remedies in India

The Constitution of India: Article 14 deals with equality. The distinction in treatment between men and women is strictly prohibited by the state based on religion, race, gender, or place of birth. Article 21 has the right to life; the right to live in human dignity.

National Women's Commission: Established as a formal body in January 1992 under the National Women's Commission Act, 1990 to review the constitution and laws to protect women; to recommend legal remedies, facilitate grievance redressal and advise Government on all policy issues affecting women.

Supreme Court Guidelines on Sexual Harassment in the Workplace: For the first time, the Court used the tool of international human rights law, CEDAW to approve a set of guidelines. The Court defined sexual harassment in the workplace as any unacceptable act, behavior, words, or sexual expression. "It shall be the duty of the employer or other persons responsible for the workplace or other institutions to prevent or prevent the conduct of sexual harassment and to provide for procedures for resolving, resolving, or prosecuting acts of sexual harassment by taking action. all necessary steps. "

Law related to violence against women includes the Indian Penal Code (IPC), civil law, and special laws. The Money Laundering Act (DPA), 1961 applies to all people, Hindus, Muslims, Christians, Parsis, and Jews. Giving, taking, or sponsoring giving or taking Dowry is a crime, which is a punishment. A few provinces (Bihar, West Bengal, Orissa, Haryana, Himachal Pradesh, and Punjab) have amended DPA to give it more teeth. The law was found to have failed to prevent evil.

When a woman's death is caused by any burn or injury or otherwise occurs under normal circumstances, within 7 years of marriage, and if it is shown that shortly before her death, she suffered cruelty or abuse by her husband or any relative. to her husband because of or in connection with any demand for Dowry, that death will be termed "death of the dock" and that husband or relative will be considered responsible for his or her death (IPC 304-B). 113-B Indian Law Act, 1872, was introduced to consider the death of Dowry.

Preventing the suicide of a child or a madman: If any person under the age of 18, any insane person, any playful person, any fool, any person in a state of intoxication, suicide, or any other person supporting the committing suicide, should. be punished with death or imprisonment or imprisonment for a period not exceeding 10 years and shall pay a fine (305 IPC). The difficulty, however, is that when a victim of a serious mental illness is shown, the benefit of the doubt is given to the respondent and he or she is released.

Suicide prevention: If any person commits suicide, anyone who supports such a suicide will be punished with imprisonment for any term of up to 10 years and will be fined (306 IPC). 113-A of the Indian Evidence Act, 1872, is related to speculation as reducing suicide. Offenses of bribery and suicide prevention are apparent, free of charge, and non-refundable.

Voluntary sexual intercourse against the natural order of any man, woman, or animal is a crime punishable by imprisonment and a fine. This provision is not applicable at all (377 IPC).

1. Other cases referred to in the IPC are: Causing a miscarriage (312 IPC), miscarriage without a woman's consent (313 IPC), death caused by an act performed to have an abortion; if the act was performed without the woman's consent (314 IPC), the act was performed to prevent the child from being born alive or cause it to die after birth (315 IPC) and depressive death of an unborn child as soon as possible in an act that could be intentional manslaughter (316 IPC).
2. The Family Courts Act, 1984: The Act was established to promote reconciliation, as well as for the immediate resolution of marital disputes and family matters.
3. Women's (Disgraceful) Representation Act, 1986: This Act prohibits the misrepresentation of women through advertisements or publications, documents, drawings, illustrations, or any other form is prohibited.
4. Commission of Sati (Prevention) Act, 1987: This Act is for the prevention and promotion of sati.
5. The Protection of Women in Domestic Violence Act, 2005, [5]was enacted to provide for the effective protection of the constitutionally guaranteed rights of women who are victims of violence of any kind. and kindness that happens in the family and related matters. It recognizes 4 types of domestic violence: physical, verbal, and emotional (including infertility, illegal marriage), and economic (including stridhan-related violence, Dowry, property), and sexual (including sexual harassment and marital rape).

According to Section 498-A of the Indian law code, 1860 -Everyone who is a spouse or relative of a woman's husband, who treats those women mercilessly shall be liable to imprisonment for a term not exceeding 3 years and with no power to fine. Section 498A of the IPC and 113A of the Evidence Act of India is enshrined in the code of law (amendment) Act, 1983. This section seeks to exempt the cruelty of newlyweds due to Dowry or other similar demands from her husband or by-laws. The above-mentioned principle was intended to cure widespread evil. As expected, the victims of such violence were women who could not ask for help from government officials to voice their grievances. in any case, social conditions family traditions, etc. prevent brides from seeking any response from government officials. Some women often abuse 498A to abuse and get their husband and wife convicted of violating this section, whose intentions and intentions are raised with baseless false accusations leveled against husbands to escape or harm the family.

In a recent landmark case- HiralHarsora v. Kusum Harsora (2016) the Supreme Court has expanded the scope of the Domestic Violence Act of 2005 by ordering the removal of the word "Old Man" from it, paving the way for the persecution of girls and even non-adults by involving women in violence and abuse. The Supreme Court has ordered the reduction of 2 of the terms (2 q4) of the Domestic Violence Act 2005. A major challenge in the laws on violence is that during the past year there has been evidence of many cases of abuse of women. provisions created for her benefit to prosecute their husbands on false charges.

LANDMARK JUDGMENTS

In the case of D. Veluswamy v. D. Patchaiammal

The Supreme Court has given a broad definition of the term "victim" under "section 2 (a) of the Domestic Violence Act" and the court further noted that all marital relations cannot be "such a relationship of" marriage to the benefit of the "Domestic Violence Act". But the victim in a lasting relationship can receive the "benefit of the action" if the five conditions imposed by the court, in this case, are proved by the relevant evidence. "The court also considered the 'final' status in this case and stated that" when a man has a 'guardian', the relationship will not be the same as marriage.

Palimony: This term was used by the court in this case and refers to maintenance grants for "women who have been living" with a man for a long time without being married and then divorced by him.

In the case entitled "Sandhya Wankhede vs. Manoj Bhimrao Wankhede ", the High Court has made a landmark decision by interpreting" Section 2 (q) of the Domestic Violence Act ". Section 2 (q) of the DV Act defines 'defendant' as "any adult male and male offender who has sought relief through this act:

It depends on whether the abusive spouse or wife living in a marital relationship can also file a complaint against a male relative or male partner ".

The High Court was questioned on the matter as in terms of Section 2 (q), a victim may "complain about an older male member, but may not complain with any female relative of her husband" or a male partner, for example, mother-in-law, mother-in-law, etc. However, in the case mentioned above, "the Supreme Court ruled that Section 2 (q) does not include the female relatives of the husband or the male partner in the meeting place. a complaint that may be lodged under the provisions of the Domestic Violence Act, 2005

MEASURES TO CONTROL AND END DOMESTIC VIOLENCE

In order to eliminate such a problem in view of the current situation, action must be taken by the women themselves. They must fight this injustice and fight for the cause that affects them the most. However, if there are obstacles along the way, there are various women's organizations and NGOs working to help women in these situations. Even the police are working very fast these days which is a good sign and there is no need to worry about women. Alternatively it would be to contact the National Women's Commission for immediate action on this matter or to set up State Commissioners in almost every province to address their grievances.

Domestic violence often has a negative impact on the victim. They are experiencing emotional, psychological, and physical changes. Domestic violence has a profound effect on victims, families, communities and their well-being. In order to stop all this, there are a variety of things to follow;

- Awareness: One of the major steps in preventing domestic violence is to make the homeowners' organization aware of the serious barriers and the consequences of domestic violence. Establish rules against domestic violence and impose severe penalties on the victim. Gather more information and educate people about the harmful effects of domestic violence. It is not right for us to ignore such things and instead raise our voices against them.
- The need for stricter laws: It is very important that the law against domestic violence should be strictly enforced. Domestic violence was recognized as a serious crime in 1983 by introducing section 498-A with the Indian finance code. This action helps to end domestic violence between family members.
- Empowered NGOs: To prevent domestic violence, individuals may also seek the help of non-governmental organizations. These organizations will make people aware of the consequences and get justice for the victim.

- Seek police assistance: If there is serious violence, people can seek legal help from the police and end domestic violence. The police play a vital role in preventing domestic violence. Special training on how to deal with domestic violence issues is provided by the police. They must regard domestic violence as a serious health issue that can cause serious damage to families.
- Be aware of the facts of domestic violence: In a flat,the owners' organization must make it obligatory for residents to learn all the facts of domestic violence. They should never ignore anyone who is a victim of domestic violence; instead, they should warn all the authorities.
- Encourage and do not intimidate: A large number of people stop when they see any form of domestic violence. This happens out of fear of injury or damage to property. People often ignore it and keep the mother from incidents like these. In such cases, it is very important to plan a meeting and encourage people to come up with solutions.
- Advice: All apartments must have a mentor who can advise people about the risk. Doing so will give people the courage to speak up when they are victims or when they see something like this.

CONCLUSION AND SUGGESTIONS

Violence against women is rampant in India. The above analysis reveals not only the increase in domestic violence (21 percent, from 15 years) in India but also the acceptance of the majority of married women (57 percent) at least one reason for forgiving a man for beating his wife. There is also a wide gap between the provinces in the increase and the acceptance of violence among women. In addition to this, it is noteworthy that there are many variables such as age, women's education, age of first marriage, racial and religious categories, women's independence, exposure to the media, women's employment status, and quality of life outside the home has a significant impact on the increase in domestic violence. However, the husbands are reported to be perpetrators of violence who show one reason or another. The reason is that women in the country are at high risk due to low levels of health which is characterized by widespread poverty, lack of education, high mortality rates among people under five years of age, poor health, high fertility rates, and high maternal mortality rates. Another factor contributing to violence against women is the perception that women have not changed much. Violence was perpetrated against women inside and outside her home.

Governments and non-governmental organizations (NGOs) are working hard to eliminate or reduce violence against women. Government efforts are in the process of enacting appropriate legislation, issuing directives, and establishing various women's welfare programs. But their implementation is still delayed, as low-level government officials are not sensitive to gender. Volunteers, on the other hand, take both preventive and response measures. But the efforts of the voluntary organizations are hampered by a lack of funding and infrastructure. A girl child education is the first step toward a better society with fewer incidents of violence. Campaigns aimed at men and boys to increase awareness and change attitudes toward gender inequality are also effective tools. As individuals and responsible citizens, we need to spread awareness and report any act of violence against women around us. For a society free of violence to be healthy the dignity of each individual must be respected. When all people are equal. Women should be treated equally to men. To achieve this goal each person regardless of gender is to contribute to his or her work. The community starts at home so each member of the household has a role to play. Domestic violence is a private matter if our people become sympathetic and begin to change their way of thinking, things will change. Expecting major changes through legislation is not possible, the law is to support and help prevent the occurrence of illegal activities. People are expected to change. In conclusion, it is, therefore, necessary for all sectors of society to contribute to ensuring a non-violent life for every woman.

CHAPTER EIGHT

ANALYSE SOCIAL MEDIATRENDS:SIGMA/ ALPHA MALEMEMES&HOW IT AIDS IN IMPOSING HEGEMONIC MASCULINITY

Author: Alan Baiju, III year of B.B.A.,LL.B. from Jindal Global Law School

Co-author: Soumik Choudhury, III year of B.B.A.,LL.B. from Jindal Global Law School

INTRODUCTION

Sigma/Alpha Male Grind set refers to a series of memes that pushes for a very skewed portrayal of 'Masculinity' and propagates the idea that men and boys should assume that they are superior, dominant, aggressive and entitled. Thereby nudging the consumers of such media to conform to a 'Hegemonic Masculinity' model wherein men who demonstrate authority, strength, bravery, confidence, competitiveness and assert their (supposed) superiority over women, enhance their general position of dominance over them (physically, intellectually, and sexually), as well as those that identify as LGBTQ+, or even those men who are deemed to be of an 'effeminate' nature. An examination of the collective portrayal of masculinity in the media, and particularly in these viral memes, has many of the same premises as a feminist framework for media studies[1] but focuses on the representation of masculinity and male identity instead. We find that, while masculine dominance is almost ubiquitous, not all masculinities relate to discourses and institutions of power in the same way. Through this paper, we aim to discuss the underlying social concept behind the representation and depiction of masculinity in the Sigma/Alpha grind set series of memes/ reels.

SIGMA/ALPHA GRINDSET: BREAKDOWN

Since the emergence of Web 2.0, this particularly toxic brand of hegemonic masculinity has gained significant traction across a range of social media and networking platforms. Popular media in general and these memes/reels, disproportionately portray men as sober, competent, authoritative, and in highly elevated 'positions'.

Since protagonist male figures have been redrawn to be tougher and separated from others, depictions of sympathy and sensitivity in males have declined. Massively popular mainstream movies such as Dabangg, American Psycho, Arjun Reddy and Die Hard often serve as the template for these memes where the leading men embody the stereotype of extreme masculinity. These memes have therefore reinforced cultural ideals of masculinity that have existed for a long timei.e.,Men are portrayed as rugged, autonomous, sexually aggressive, fearless, ruthless, fully in charge of all emotions [except for anger], and most importantly, not feminine. We also find it equally interesting how males are not presented; Men are rarely portrayed performing housework or tending to others, and they are frequently shown as disinterested in and inept at domestic duties, cooking, and childcare, Adding to the unfavourable impression of males as indifferent and uncommitted in their families.

While this trend bears some parallels to antifeminismwhich has and continues to remain in popular media, by operationalizing tropes of victimhood, "beta males," and its contrast with so-called "real men" or Alpha males, these new toxic assemblages further convolutesthe pre-existing traditional structures of dominance and power. These memes raise crucial concerns about how male hegemony functions both offline and online, indicating that social media's technological attributes are particularly well suited to propagating new assertions of what it supposedly means to be a "real man /alpha male".

ANALYSIS

We believe that the underlying social concept behind the representation and depiction of masculinity in the Sigma/Alpha grind set series of memes/ reels is Hegemonic Masculinity.

Hegemonic masculinity depicts the hierarchical interaction between numerous masculinities and explains how certain men make it appear natural and necessary for them to dominate most women and other men.[2] Hegemonic masculinity is a notion that helps us understand how the presence of several masculinities creates hierarchical dominance not just between men and women, but also within males. The notion of hegemonic masculinity was first proposed in the 1980s to characterize a set of social practices that favoured and promoted men's social status over that of women's. It is based on the existence of a dominant form of masculinity.Men generally tend to situate themselves in reference to it and as a result, internalise personal standards of behaviour that help to perpetuate it. The need to adhere to and relate to this ideal hegemonic masculinity has supplemented in maintaining society's gender-based hierarchy. It is the extension of this very concept that has manifested in the portrayal of "masculinity "in the sigma/ alpha grind set memes/reels.

This concept ties into the argument that R.W Connell presents; "that men enact and embody different configurations of masculinity depending on their positions within a social hierarchy of power"[3] under this model, he categorises different configurations.

HEGEMONIC MASCULINITY & ALPHA MALES

As explained above, Hegemonic masculinity is the type of gender practice that, in a given space and time, supports gender inequality, and is at the top of this hierarchy. Parallels to this gender practice may be drawn to the portrayal of "Alpha males/real men '' as portrayed in the meme format, such males are depicted to be at the apex of the social status hierarchy. Owing to their physical prowess, intimidation, and domination these men often have easier access to power, money, and partners. As Connell observes, such a type of identity is neither easy to achieve nor necessarily desirable in and of itself; rather, it is a collection of prescribed and glorified ideals rather than an accurate depiction of men's lived realities. Hegemonic masculinity, on the other hand, provides a normative standard to which men might aspire and against which they can evaluate their own identities.

SUBORDINATE MASCULINITY & BETA MALES

Subordinate modes of masculinity, which exist outside of the acceptable forms of maleness as portrayed in the hegemonic form and are controlled, oppressed, and subordinated and there stands stark in contrast to hegemonic masculinity.The hegemonic form is inextricably linked to subordinated masculinities, and it is necessary for it to develop subordinate forms in order to maintain the hierarchical structure[4].We discover that masculinities are built-in contradistinction to femininity; and therefore, those at the bottom of the male hierarchy will be symbolically assimilated to femininity and tend to share similar traits with the "feminine" forms[5].The two strategies of subordination may be broadly put into two generic headings of "difference" and/or "deficit". Being different from most the dominant majority is an unenviable situation to be in, and the "peer group culture's " intense demands to conformity mean that a male would only have to look and act slightly different from the norm to be assigned inferior status[6]. Males under the bracket of subordinated masculinity are associated closely with, speaking too formally, being excessively cooperative or overpolite. This depiction bears true to the sigma/ grind set memes where the so-called "beta males" are depicted as a man who lacks societally perceived and accepted "masculine" traits and adopts "feminine" characteristics and appearances and often faces problems or confrontations passive-aggressively. These atypical physical appearances and differences in the body language of "beta males" are acutely commented on. The second heading is “deficit,” wherein subordination comes through perceived exhibitions of “immature” and “infantile” behaviour, displaying a deficit or deficiency of toughness (for instance not being assertive, or acting ‘soft’) anda lack of some culturally praised characteristics, especially those associated with embodied types of physique and athletic prowessall of which are used as a marker of difference.

As hegemonic masculinity is based on the perpetuation of patriarchy and heterosexuality, gay or trans men who defy heterosexual norms are also viewed as exemplifying subordinated kinds of masculinity. In patriarchal ideology, gayness serves as a repository for all that is symbolically excluded from hegemonic masculinity[7]. Due to the prevalent cultural stigmatization of homosexual individuals, this system often deems gay men as outcasts as they are not "real men". Many seemingly harmless remarks such as "Man up" or "Don’t do that, what are you, a faggot?" are acts of active gender policing in which the fear of subordination, loss of legitimacy, and complicity is actively implemented.

MARGINALIZED MASCULINITIES

Marginalized Masculinities examines how men in precarious positions in many countries and social circumstances interpret and experience their masculinities, with a focus on males who are marginalised in a variety of areas such as family, employment, race, the media, and school. The interaction of gender with other structures such as class and race leads to further intricacies within Intra- masculine relationships, hence race relations also becomes an important aspect of the masculinity dynamics. Marginalised masculinity, therefore, refers to the masculinities in dominant and subjugated social classes or ethnic groups. Marginalization is always linked to the ruling group's authorization of hegemonic masculinity. The fact that disadvantaged masculinities pose a threat to hegemonic masculinity is the primary reason for their suppression. Any purportedly natural nonconformity, particularly with relation to gender, is a danger to hegemonic masculinity. The nature of dominant discourse is to present itself as all there is, as "natural," and "normal." Black homosexuals threaten the Euro-Americans' definition of normality-for they "are not white, male, or heterosexual and generally not affluent" [8]. 'Hegemonic masculinity and 'marginalized masculinities' are not permanent character types, but rather practice configurations formed in specific settings within a shifting relationship system.[9] . Exhibition of marginalised masculinity does make several appearances in the Alpha/ sigma memes wherein there are disturbing portrayals of white supremacy and other racist undertones tied into these memes. Furthermore, the class distinction in this meme series is very evident, "alpha/sigma males" are projected as overachieving wealthy and successful upper echelon males often depicted using the image macros of actors and models in lavish suits living larger than life lifestyles while "beta males" are often portrayed as financially unstable and unproductive.

INTERSECTIONALITY IN MASCULINE CONFIGURATIONS

People identify with multiple social groups and their co-existence and contribution to identity are complex, as social categories mesh and intersect with each other. The theory of intersectionality[10] recognizes this complexity and presents a useful framework for assessing an overlap that we have recognised between race (classified under marginalised masculinity) and sexuality (classified under subordinate masculinity). In such instances of intersection like that of homosexualAfrican American men, individuals are disadvantaged by multiple sources of oppression based on different social groups that exist within an identity. An insight into the oppression due to this intersection is observed in the way Lil Nas X, a popular American rapper, recounts his childhood in an interview in 2019 after he came out as being homosexual. "Growing up in the Atlanta area, I [saw] a lot of microaggressions towards homosexuality," he told Tre'vell Anderson. "Little things like going into an IHOP and hearing one of your family members say 'look at those faggots' to two people eating or even just a small [statement like] ‘boys don’t cry.’ Little things like living in the hood, not being super into sports, and then having to go outside and pretend that I was.”[11] Post revealing his sexuality Lil Nas X also received widespread backlash and the whole ordeal made its way into popular memes in various offensive meme formats.

CONCLUSION

Combating the perpetuation of hegemonic masculinity is imperative to confining any further development of socially constructed and stereotypical narratives of the differences between males and females. This type of gender socialisation reinforces dominance and subjugation between both Intra and Inter-gender roles. The first step is to recognise the societal implications of hegemonic masculinity. We can then bring about societal change by comprehending them and promoting the establishment of true, full gender equality between and within genders.

The notion of hegemonic masculinity is only as good as its conception of man. Domination occurs not only between genders but also within genders. The root of the problem, therefore, is not man in general, but specific toxic behaviours connected with dominance and power which affect both men and women alike. This fosters a relationship of mutual understanding and solidarity between men and women, potentially leading to a shift in gender attitudes. Promoting public reasoning processes and debates about the implications of hegemonic masculinities' marginalisation and disempowerment could be one approach to possibly lead to a positive shift in gender attitudes and redefining gender perceptions, thereby paving the way to a more equitable society.

CHAPTER NINE

COPYRIGHT - AN ABSOLUTE RIGHTWITH A FAIR USE DEFENCE

Author: P.Lavanya, B.A.,B.L.(Hons)., LLM., Ph.D from The Tamilnadu Dr. Ambedkar Law University, Chennai.

Lavanya

INTRODUCTION

A person may make limited use of the original author's work without asking permissionUnder the "fair use" defence. Certain copy righted uses are not an infringement which is"for the purposes of criticism, comment, news reporting, teaching (including multiple copies for classroom use), scholarship, or research. It is purely based on the matter of policy that the public is entitled to freely use portions of copyrighted materials. Before moving into defence rule let's see what copyright is, fair use and it'sinfringement.

COPYRIGHT

Copyright is nothing but the exclusive and assignable legal rightfor a fixed number of years which is given to the originator to print, publish, perform, film, or record literary, artistic, or musical material.

INFRINGEMENT

The copyright is infringed when other than the legal owner usesthe works without permission, protected by copyright law infringing certain exclusive rights granted to the copyright holder, such as the right to reproduce, distribute, display or perform the protected work, or to make derivative works. The copyright holder is typically the work's creator, or a publisher or other business to whom copyright has been assigned. Copyright holders routinely invoke legal and technological measures to prevent and penalize copyright infringement.

Copyright infringement disputes are usually resolved through direct negotiation, a notice and take down process, or litigation in civil court. Egregious or large-scale commercial infringement, especially when it involves counterfeiting, is sometimes prosecuted via the criminal justice system. Shifting public expectations, advances in digital technology, and the increasing reach of the Internet have led to such widespread, anonymous infringement that copyright-dependent industries now focus less on pursuing individuals who seek and share copyright-protected content online, and more on expanding copyright law to recognize and penalize - as "indirect" infringers - the service providers and software distributors which are said to facilitate and encourage individual acts of infringement by others.

Estimates of the actual economic impact of copyright infringement vary widely and depend on many factors. Nevertheless, copyright holders, industry representatives, and legislators have long characterized copyright infringement as "piracy" or "theft" - language which some U.S. courts now regard as pejorative or otherwise contentious.[1]In Pine Labs Private Limited vs Gemalto Terminals India Limited[2] a division bench of the Delhi High Court confirmed this position and held that in cases wherein the duration of assignment is not specified, the duration shall be deemed to be five years and the copyright shall revert to the author after five years.

LIABILITY OR PERMISSIBLE FAIR USE

The World Wide Web is a "hypertext" medium, allowing web site creators to easily insert "jump links" to any other pages on the Internet. It was surely inevitable that disputes would arise about the permissible scope of this activity. In fact, people who have objected to finding a link to their web page on some website they deem unsavory for one reason or another.In an instance, a woman who placed a picture of her recently deceased daughter on a web page in honor of her memory, found it linked from a site labeled "Babes on the Net." Many of these disputes have been resolved informally. Nevertheless, eventually, as more money became involved, some disputants would turn to more expensive forms of dispute resolution (i.e., to litigation).

And sure enough, hyper linking is at the heart of two recent lawsuits involving some pretty high-profile players. In one, a group of news organizations including CNN, Reuters, Time, and the Wall Street Journal has sued an Interne tope ration known as Total News. TotalNews.com is a website that brings together links to a variety of sources of news on the Web. Thus, by going to the Total News site, a user can find a page with a set of links to other websites providing political news (C-Span, The Economist, etc.), sports news (ESP Net, Fox Sports, etc.), and the like. Plaintiffs are objecting to having their web sites included on that set of links.

The defendant in the second suit is none other than Microsoft Corporation, which (among other things) runs, Seattle.Sidewalk.Com a city guide with information about upcoming events in the Seattle area. For those events that require tickets, Seattle. Sidewalk informs you that you may be able to purchase tickets through Ticketmaster (and it both provides some information about Ticketmaster's operations and a link to the Ticket master website). Ticketmaster, like the news organizations involved in the Total News dispute, has filed suit in federal district court to try to prevent this.

Now, why would CNN, or Time, or Ticketmaster, object to a link to their pages? Isn't the whole point of having a web page to attract users? These hyperlinks are like referrals and one rarely hears of one party suing another for sending customers to their store. What's going on here?

In a word advertising (and advertising dollars). In both suits, plaintiffs are asserting that the way that defendants link to their page deprives the plaintiffs of advertising revenuethat is properly theirs. Total News, for example, surrounds its web page with a "frame" -- a border that appears on the screen that contains advertising sold by Total News (or other messages that Total News wants you to see). Things get interesting now: if, say, you click on the link to ABC's web page, you will indeed see the ABC page but the Total News border continues to sit there, showing you the advertising that Total News has sold (which squeezes any advertising that ABC may contain into a smaller area on your screen). Similarly, Ticketmaster asserts that Microsoft, by linking to the Ticketmaster website, "has gained revenue from advertising made a part of Microsoft's website, depriving Ticketmaster of favorable advertising business" and that its actions constitute "electronic piracy."

These cases thus present the rather intriguing question: Does the law grant website operators any control over the manner in which individual hyperlinks to their site can be constructed? As the Ticketmaster and Total News cases (and the others that no doubt will follow) begin their journey through the legal system, two things are noteworthy at the outset.

First is the way in which this question illuminates the way in which Internet legal questions are (and are not) "new." If you think about it a bit, the real world is full of hyperlinks; a footnote in an article, or an entry in a book index, is a kind of hyperlink, as is a business' telephone number listed at the bottom of an advertisement. The telephone book itself is nothing more than a collection of hyperlinks, and even a familiar commercial logo the golden arches, for example functions as a kind of "hyperlink" to a "database" of information about specific companies that consumers carry around with them in their heads.

Precisely because hyper linking (of a sort) appears as a (small) part of so many different activities, there's lots of law scattered about the legal landscape governing hyper linking activity. Many legal doctrines trademark law, copyright law, and unfair competition, and privacy, misrepresentation touch upon different aspects of the question regarding the extent to which hyper linking-type activity is, or is not, permissible. However, there has never been a need to gather it together into a coherent theory of hyper linking or a coherent legal doctrine neatly labeled "The Permissible Scope of Hyper linking." But in the face of a medium whose very existence and viability is defined by its hyper linking capabilities, courts will have to do just that, drawing these disparate strands and fragments together into some sort of coherent whole. Litigation, of course, is an imperfect vehicle for constructing coherent doctrine. Plaintiffs will undoubtedly throw in as many different claims from as many of these pre-existing legal pigeonholes as they can, from relatively well-defined trademarkinfringement claims to the more "flexible" doctrines like commercial misappropriation and unfair competition and see what sticks. But slowly, over the course of many such suits and court decisions, a sensible framework may indeed emerge.

But slowly is the operative word. It's important to note that these two lawsuits have something else in common: both involve problems for which there is relatively simple technology 'fixes.' Ticketmaster can easily program its site to prohibit access to anyone coming in from Seattle.sidewalk.com, and, similarly, any news organizations can insert a few lines of code in its website program to prevent Total News from retaining its frames around the site. (Some, in fact, have already done so; if you're interested, go to Total News and explore the link to the New York Times website and presto! the Total News frame disappears). So, you might ask yourself: if your client wants to protect its website against this framing actively, will it turn to its techies, or its lawyers, to be the first line of defense?

So while the legal system plods on, we're probably going to see a kind of technological "arms race" involving these (and perhaps most) Internet property disputes. Technology can take the away what it give; Total News will undoubtedly come up with a few lines of code of its own to defeat the Times' efforts, the Times will then respond with another trick, and on and on it will go. And this will all happen on "Internet time" - the time frame of response and counter-response will be compressed and foreshortened, and independent of the comparatively glacial pace of legal change. By the time the courts get around to providing an authoritative determination regarding the "right" of website owners to control linking to their sites, the technology of linking will probably look nothing like what we see today, and we may have long forgotten the conduct that started these disputes. The role of the courtroom as a place where rules of conduct are constructed may be substantially undermined in this context. Military officers are often derided for planning to fight the previous war why do we lawyers face a similar fate?

LIMITATIONS ON EXCLUSIVE RIGHTS

Fair Use Not every act of copying constitutes copyright infringement. The doctrine of "fair use" permits certain acts of copying. Under the doctrine, criticism, news reporting, teaching, and scholarly comment are all fair uses of copyrighted works. Appeals focusing on the defense of fair use to a claim of copyright infringement have reached The Supreme Court of the United States three times since 1984. In each of these cases, the holding of the lower court was overturned. It i s not unfair to say that fair use is the most troublesome doctrine in the whole of copyright law. The copyright statute which has incorporated this doctrine states that in determining whether the use made of a work in any particular case is a fair use the factors to be considered shall include:

1. the purpose and character of the use, including whether such use is of a commercial nature or is for nonprofit educational purposes;
2. the nature of the copyrighted work;
3. the amount and substantiality of the portion used in relation to the copyrighted work as a whole; and
4. the effect of the use upon the potential market for or value of the copyrighted work

CHAPTER TEN

DOES FOREIGN TRADE AFFECT THE ECONOMY OF OUR COUNTRY?

Author: P.Lavanya, B.A.,B.L.(Hons)., LLM., Ph.D from The Tamilnadu Dr. Ambedkar Law University, Chennai.

Lavanya

ABSTRACT

India's economic structure today presents a distinctly different picture from what it was in 1991 when economic reforms started. In 1991 our foreign exchange reserves had depleted substantially. We then had just enough reserves to tide over the import requirements of three weeks. It was in this context that India gradually started dismantling its quantitative restrictions, partially liberalised its exchange rate and reduced the peak rate of customs duties. More importantly, this sector was overly dependent on western markets and, consequently, extremely vulnerable to even the smallest of developments there. The policy, fortunately, turns its attention to other sectors where India has inherent advantages – healthcare, education, R&D, logistics, professional services, entertainment, as well as services incidental to manufacturing. By extending benefits under EPCG on domestic procurements and offering them more products under MEIS, the policy further seeks to incentives the for the exports. The average duty on all products stands reduced from over 70% in 1991-92 to 12% in 2008-09. However, at the same time the whole world was rushing towards globalisation and integration. Had India not joined the race, the economic scenario could have worsened. The only recourse left to India was to increase its exports to tide over the ever-increasing imports. We were aiming to gain a considerable proportion of international business and make our presence felt on the international front.

INTRODUCTION

As we can see, e-commerce plays a very significant role in today's trade the Government announced various export promotion measures and incentives. Laws were framed to streamline the process of export and import. These laws ensured that our commitment to expansion of India's trade remained firm. The laws and facilitations announced by the Government were not only related to export and import of goods and services but were also directed to upgradation of technology and integration of all the departments by using latest technologies available. According to some experts the focus in this FTP has been "Simplicity and Stability". Accordingly, the policy on the one hand seeks to realign the multiple schemes with the objective of reducing complexities. On the other had it want to promote the increased use of technology to reduce the transaction cost and manual compliances.

Supporters have given their verdict for this new FTP, stating it as 'progressive', 'path breaking' and 'development friendly' as exports of books, handicraft, handlooms, toys, textiles, defence and ecommerce platforms would be easier and faster. According to them, a big step is cleaning up the plethora of export promotion schemes andclubbing them under two schemes, one for goods (Merchandise Exports from India

Scheme) and one for services (Services Exports from India Scheme).The duty scrips under these schemes come without conditions and can be freely transferred. One significant announcement in the policy is that it will move away from relying largely on subsidies and sops. Critics however point out that, this is prompted by World Trade Organization (WTO) requirements that export promotion subsidies should be phased out, but according to some experts there are ways of getting around it and other countries are doing it all the time. There has been talk of boosting services exports for quite a few years now, but information technology and information technology-enabled services (IT/ITES) dominated the basket. The share of this segment in the overall export basket is 50 percent and 90 percent in the services export basket.

According to the Commerce Minister Nirmala Sitaraman, It's a focused policy, one in which exports through Make in India is underlined by looking at sectors that give greater employment and have high-tech value addition. That is because the intention is to join the global value chain and above all, the environment part, where you are looking at eco-friendly systems and producing wealth out of waste. So, the priority areas are technology-driven, labour-intensive-driven and environment-driven. You are also looking at traditional markets, emerging markets and diversifying into new markets.

HOW EXIM POLICY AFFECTS THE ECONOMY OF OUR COUNTRY?

The important disadvantages of foreign trade are listed below,

1. Impediment in the Development of Home Industries: Foreign trade has an adverse effect on the development of home industries. It poses a threat to the survival of infant industries at home. Due to foreign competition and unrestricted imports the upcoming industries in the country may collapse.
2. Economic Dependence: The underdeveloped countries have to depend upon the developed ones for their economic development. Such reliance often-leads to economic exploitation. For, instance most of the underdeveloped countries in Africa and Asia have been exploited by European countries.
3. Political Dependence: Foreign trade often encourages subjugation and slavery. It impairs economic independence which endangers political dependence. For example, the Britishers came to India as traders and ultimately ruled over India for a very long time.

4. Mis-utilization of Natural resources: Excessive exports may exhaust the natural resources of a country in a shorter span of time than it would have been otherwise. This will cause economic downfall of the country in the long run.
5. Import of Harmful Goods: Import of spurious drugs, Luxury articles, etc. adversely affects the economy and well being of the people.
6. Storage of Goods: Sometimes the essential commodities required in a country and in short supply are also exported to earn foreign exchange. This results in shortage of these goods at home and cause inflation. For example, India has been exporting sugar to earn foreign exchange; hence the exalting prices of sugar in the country
7. Danger to Internal Peace: Foreign trade gives an opportunity to foreign agents to settle down in the country which ultimately endangers its internal peace.
8. World Wars: Foreign trade breeds rivalries amongst nations due to competition in the foreign markets. This may event fully lead to wars and disturbs world peace.
9. Hardships in times of wars: Foreign trade promotes lopsided development of a country as only those goods which have comparative cost advantage are produced in a country. During wars or when good relations do not prevail between nations, many hardships may follow.

IMPACT ON EFFICIENCY AND GROWTH

- Optimal use of natural resources: Foreign trade helps each country to make optimum use of its natural resources. Each country can concentrate on production of those goods for which its resources are best suited. Wastage of resources is avoided.
- Availability of all type of goods: It enables a country to obtain goods, which it cannot produce or which it is not producing due to higher costs, by importing from other countries at lower costs.
- Specialisation: Foreign trade leads to specialization and encourages production of different good in different countries. Goods can be produced at comparatively low cost due to advantages of division of labour.
- Advantages of large-scale production: Due to foreign trade, goods are produced not only for home consumption but for exports to other countries also. Nations of the world can dispose of goods which they

have in surplus in the foreign markets. This leads to production at large-scale and the advantages of large-scale production can be obtained by all the countries of the world.

- Stability in prices: Foreign trade irons out wild, fluctuations in prices. It equalizes the prices of goods throughout the world (ignoring cost of transportation etc.).
- Exchange of technical know-how and establishment of new industries: Underdeveloped countries can establish and develop new industries with the machinery equipment and technical know-how imported from developed countries. This helps in the development of these countries and the economy of the world at large.
- Increase in efficiency: Due to the foreign competition the producers in a country attempt to produce better quality of goods and at the minimum possible cost. This increases the efficiency and benefits the consumers all over the world.
- Development of the means of transport and communications: Foreign trade requires the best means of transport and communication. For the advantages of foreign trade development in the means of transport and communication is also made possible.
- International co-operation and understanding: The people of different countries come in contact with each other. Commercial intercourse amongst nations of the world encourages exchange of ideas and culture. It creates co-operation, understanding and cordial relations amongst various nations
- Ability to face natural calamities: Natural calamities such as drought, floods, famine, earthquake etc., affect the production of a country adversely. Deficiency in the supply of goods at the times of such natural calamities can be met by imports from other countries.
- Other advantages: Foreign trade helps in many other ways such as benefits to consumers, international peace and better standard of living.

ECONOMIC (TRADE) REFORMS IN INDIA

In order to understand the evolution of the Foreign trade policy (EXIM policy) over time we need to understand the larger framework and evolution of Macroeconomic policy in India before and after the liberalisation in the 90's. The subsequent trade policies were developed keeping in view this larger framework and in sequence to it.

In the early eighties, the Government of India appointed a special EXIM Policy Committee to review the government previous export import policies. The committee was later on approved by the Government of India. Mr. V. P. Singh, the then Commerce Minister and announced the EXIM Policy on April, 1985. Initially the EXIM Policy was introduced for the period of three years with main objective to boost the export business in India.

Now, let us understand the history and evolution of foreign trade policy in India we need to understand it under different phases of Policy in Practice: Trends in Foreign Trade Policy 1950 -1990: India entered into planned development era in 1950's and at that time Import Substitution was a major element of India's trade and industrial policy. In 1950 India's share in the total world trade was 1.78% which reduced to 0.6% in 1995. During 2003-04 India's share in the global trade was 0.8%, in 2005 it was 1.0%.

The PC Alexander Committee (1978) was the first committee to review and recommend on Import –Export Policies and Procedures. This committee recommended the simplification of the Import Licensing procedure and provided a framework involving a shift in the emphasis from "control to development". In 1980 Tandon Committee gave recommendations on export strategies in eighties.

In the Export Import policy of 1978-79, for the first time in India's History decentralization of some licensing functions took place and the powers of regional licensing authorities was enhanced. Export Oriented Units were set up under the EOU scheme introduced in early 1981. The export and Import Bank of India (website) was set up in 1982 to take over the operations of international finance wing of the IDBI. Other major objectives was to provide financial assistance to exporters and importers.

In the Trade Policy of 1985-88 some measures were taken based upon the recommendation of Abid Husain Committee 1984. This committee envisaged "Growth Led Exports, rather than Export Led Growth". The recommendation of this committee stressed upon the need for harmonizing the foreign trade policies with other domestic policies. This committee recommended announcement of foreign trade policies for longer terms.

The export import pass book scheme was introduced in 1985 as per recommendation of Abid Hussain Committee. In 1985 Vishvanathpratap Singh Government developed a 3 yearexim policy.Tax Reform Committee chaired by Raja J. Chelliah suggested minimizing the role of quantitative restrictions and reducing the tariff rates substantially. Export Processing

Zones were set up to push up exports. They are now SEZ.

MAIN FEATURES OF TRADE POLICIES- ERA OF REFORMS

As discussed the massive trade liberalisation measures adopted after 1991 mark a major departure from the relatively protectionist trade policies pursued in earlier years. Accordingly, Substantial simplification and liberalisation has been carried out in the reform period. Foreign Trade Policy (FTP) or Export Import Policy (EXIM) is believed to be an important step towards the economic reforms of India. In order to liberalize imports and boost exports, the Government of India for the first time introduced the Indian EXIM Policy on April I, 1992.

In the light of the reform policy objectives successive governments have been taking various trade reforms. Successive annual Union Budgets have also extended a number of tax benefits and exemptions to the exporters. These include reduction in the peak rate of customs duty to 15 per cent; significant reduction in duty rates for critical inputs for the Information Technology sector, which is an important export sector; grant of concessions for building infrastructure by way of 10-years tax holiday to the developers of SEZs; Facilities and tax benefits to exporters of goods and merchandise; reduction in the customs duty on specified equipment for ports and airports to 10 per cent to encourage the development of world class infrastructure facilities, etc. A number of tax benefits have also been announced for the three integral parts of the 'convergence revolution' the Information Technology sector, the Telecommunication sector, and the Entertainment industry.

In order to bring stability and continuity, the Export Import Policy was made for the duration of 5 years. However, the Central government reserves the right in public interest to make any amendments to the trade Policy in exercise of the powers conferred by Section-5 of the Act. Such amendment shall be made by means of a Notification published in the Gazette of India.

Prior to 2004, the Foreign Trade Policy was called EXIM Policy. Each FTP will be having objectives and set guidelines to achieve those objectives. After the introduction of liberalisation in Indian economy, 1992-97 policy was the first EXIM Policy which aimed to dismantle the protectionist and regulatory policy towards a globally oriented economy.

GOVERNMENT INITIATIVES IN IMPORTS AND EXPORTS

To encourage exports, the Government of India has offered a number of incentives. The export-import policy announced by the government every year specifies the details of export assistance and incentives. Some of the important incentives are given below

Import Replenishment (REP) Licenses Under this scheme, the exporters are allowed to import raw materials and components used in the manufacture of export products. The policy contains a list of items of import for which REPs are to be granted. Deemed exporters are also granted REP license. Deemed exports mean, producers who supply the inputs to final exporters. They are considered as indirect exporters and are eligible for certain export benefits. Certain supplies of import substitution are also termed as deemed exports. They qualify for grant of REP but not other benefits. In India, When there was an import restriction earlier, the Import Replenishment licenses were sold at a premium. Now, with liberalization of imports, the scheme is no longer attractive. The holder of REP license is permitted to import canalized items, capital goods, samples and tools.

Import – Export Pass Book Scheme This scheme enables, the Export House, Trading Houses and manufacturer — exporters having good track record of exports, to import duty free raw materials. The scheme has extended its coverage even to well-established manufacturers.

Duty Exemption Scheme Duty exemption scheme allows the duty free import of certain components, raw materials, consumables and spares for export production. It covers categories of advance license, blanket advance license and advance customs clearance permits. It provides benefits to indirect exporters. The license holder of this scheme is also eligible for REP license.

100% Export Oriented Units These units are exempted from import licensing formalities. They are allowed to import capital goods, raw materials, components, consumables and spares under the Open General License on the condition that their entire production should be exported and operations are carried out under customs bonded factory. A 100% export oriented unit can be set up in Free Trade Zones (FTZs), promoted by Government with infrastructure facilities. Examples are Madras Export Processing Zone (MEPZ), Santacruz Electronic Processing Zone (SEPZ), besides similar zones are in Kandla (Gujarat), Noida (Delhi), Cochin. Units in FTZ and 100% Export oriented units have been given special status. Under Income Tax Act, there is complete tax holiday for 5 years for these units. The EOU/EPZ scheme has been liberalized to include units which export 50% of their production for agriculture, aquaculture, horticulture, floriculture, animal husbandry, poultry and sericulture units. The taxation system spells out a number of benefits to small-scale industries. Various tax benefits are available to small business units, both at the Centre and State level. The Central government levies direct taxes, whereas indirect taxes are levied by the State government. State government provides benefits in sales tax, water tax, octroi duty and electricity tariff, etc.

Tax exemption on earnings The profits earned on export earnings are deducted by 50% for calculation of tax. It can be availed of by an individual or company. There are also deductions available for earnings in foreign exchange by approved hotels or travel agents. There is a provision of deduction in respect of expenditure incurred by the companies for promoting sales outside India

Exemption of Sales Tax There is an exemption from sales tax, excise duty and import duty for exports. Exemption of excise duty can be obtained by way of rebate or duty drawback. When the exports earning are negative, no duty drawback is paid on claims.

Cash assistance to exporters Cash assistance is given to enable exporters to compete in the international market. It is given as a percentage on the FOB value of exports. There is International Price Reimbursement Scheme. This scheme is designed to match the differences in the international prices of steel, aluminium, pig iron, etc.

Liberalized Exchange Rate Management System (LERMS) Under Liberalized Exchange Rate Management System, the Government allows partial convertibility of rupee for all the approved transactions. In this system, exporters of goods and services who receive remittances from abroad would be able to sell bulk of their foreign exchange receipts at market determined rates from the authorized dealers.

Export Promotion Capital Goods Scheme (EPCG) This scheme permits the import of capital goods at a concessional rate of customs duty, subject to export obligation to be fulfilled over a period of time. The scheme is applicable to service sector also. Second hand capital goods are allowed to be imported under certain conditions. The importer has to obtain the EPCG licence. The capital goods cannot be sold for 5 years. Small industries can import capital goods through National Small Industries Corporation of India Ltd (NSIC) and State Small Industries Corporation (SSIC). Application for imports of capital goods, raw materials, components and consumables should be routed through the DIC.

CONCLUSION

The year of 1991 was momentous, in the economy, in the history of India as it witnessed a successful transition of India from a controlled and slow-growing economy to a liberalized and open economy that has now found a country amongst the fastest growing economies in the world. When the Indian economy was opened to external competition, Indian industry was emerging much stronger to find its rightful entity not only in the domestic market but also in international market. The process of planned economic development in India began with the launching of First Five Year Plan in April, 1951. Today, the Government has the Eleventh Five Year Plan (2007-12) In short, over the last 65 years, India's Foreign Trade has undergone a complete change in terms of composition and direction. The Government of India introduced a series of reforms to liberalize and globalize the Indian economy Reform of Foreign Trade was a critical element in structural reform as well as economic reform. Today, the destination pattern of Indian Foreign Trade has remarkably changed, in the sense that the significance of developing countries as Foreign Trade has considerable increased. All EXIM polices or FTPs in India regard to liberalization and globalization of the Foreign Trade has witnessed very significant change.

CHAPTER ELEVEN

IS CONSTITUTION REALLY PROTECTING RIGHT TO PRIVACY IN CYBER SPACE?

Author: Nikunj Pandey, III year of B.Com.,LL.B. from Institute of Law, Nirma University, Ahmedabad

Co-author: Mumal Kunwar Bhati, III year of B.Com.,LL.B. from Institute of Law, Nirma University, Ahmedabad

Introduction

Right to Privacy means "right to live alone, right to be free from any unwarranted interference"[1]. In India, development of privacy as a right could be traced back to plethora of cases where right to privacy was in question; however none of the cases could give privacy its due importance. Further, in 2017, K.S. Puttaswamy judgment[2] fueled the spark that was going on for years, which declared privacy as a fundamental right under Indian Constitution and hence it became as important as any other fundamental right. But the question that arises "Is constitution really protecting Right to Privacy in cyber space?"

Today, we are living in the technologically possessed world; with the advent of technology it had brought revolution in the lives of people. Everything is available at a mouse click from shopping to study, from food to travel etc. However, in the ease of doing transaction we are not realizing that after disseminating all our details on the online platform we are paving way for the criminals to creep into our privacy.

The right is available but there are no sufficient remedies to protect this right, this is evident from the rampant increase in cyber crimes across India and there lies the major challenges before the Government to fill the gaps in the existing legislation.

Cyber crime and right to privacy

The right to privacy is a crucial natural requirement of every human being since it establishes boundaries around an individual, limiting other people's access. Accessing the personal or proprietary information of a person illegally and without his/her permission amounts to breach of right to privacy.

Cybercrime infringes the human rights of freedom of speech and expression, right to privacy, freedom of opinion and free flow of information. As cyber security threats are becoming increasingly widespread, complex and intense the breach of such human rights will grow. The cyber security issues are directly and substantially privacy and data security issues. With the recent revolution of social media and smart technologies, threats related to information security are elevating. Huge chunks of private data are left open to cyber attacks as firms struggle to stay up with the shifting landscape created by innovative technologies social practices and ever changing risks.

It becomes a matter of worry that though guaranteed by the Indian constitution as fundamental rights, there is no proper remedy available to protect our privacy.

Challenges to cyber security

Technology in creases risks of cybercrimes

Large-scale initiatives like Digital India with the 2nd largest internet users[3] globally offers dramatic progress but this revolution of technology is exposing our society to newer and bigger fundamental threats. Although such technological advancements leading us to a better future but at the cost of our privacy.

The new-age technologies like IoTs, AIs & cloud services are accumulating more and more data from individuals, Business entities, Government at one place, making it more vulnerable by opening up window for cyber crooks to commit significantly bigger, more lucrative cyber attacks.

This enormous data of general public stored with various organizations consists personal information such as fingerprints, sexual orientation, job profile, family details, living standards etc., it is vexatious to not have any dedicated law for the protection of our privacy.

Threats to cyber security will only intensify as the technology advances and no. of internet user increases. It has now become a norm today to allow the social media platforms to access, retain & process our personal data to sell it for targeted advertisements and other purpose. We have risked our privacy to access their services and as a consequence they now possess information like our location to daily activities, from the hotel we checked in to our photos. The breach of such information contends to serious infringement of our privacy.

Technology-powered increase in cybercrime[4]

1. Artificial Intelligence (AI) / Machine Learning (ML)

AI is a discipline that attempts to build smart systems and explore techniques for resolving complicated issues which are supposed to be solved by human thought, reasoning and judgment abilities.

ML is the study of building advanced software applications, that can constantly self upgrade or enhance their performance by experience. These technologies are deployed in a no. of industries to improve the efficiency and scalability of systems.

AI/ML poses potentially bigger threats to the data of different individuals, groups, and organizations by increasing the frequency, efficiency, volume and automation of attacks.

2. IoT and cyber crime

Cybercrime's threat landscape has been widening as devices, sensory systems, appliances and cameras which constitute the IoTs continue to rise in numbers. By 2025, 41.6 billion linked IoT devices (or "things") will be producing 79.4 Zettabytes (ZB) of data as per the projections of International Data Corporation[5].

Data acquired by IOT devices is becoming increasingly prone to theft, corruption, obliteration, coercion ad trade. It introduces new risks in existing IT systems and environments by widening the attack surface for cybercrime.

3. Privacy enhancing technologies PETs

Cyber crooks could deploy the PETs to commit illicit activities making it more difficult to track and investigate such criminal acts. Such technology could also be used to gain access to private information.

- Data accumulation: causing serious threat

Data is the new oil

– Mukesh Ambani

As we walk through different websites to shop, book doctors' appointment or pay the bills. A digital profile has been created of our private information, which is left vulnerable to theft and other cyber crimes that amounts to breach of privacy.

With the steady advancements of Artificial Intelligence, social media and e-commerce platforms, this digital profile of our private data is not only retained but further used for other monetary purposes. In 2018, the Facebook-Cambridge Analytica[6] case drew the attention of several nations to the protection of their citizens' privacy.

Big data analytics contends that it could be used in detecting cyber risks at an early stage by employing advanced analysis methods. Big data can be equipped in enhancing public safety and security measures and can play a vital role as a problem solving too. On the other hand it brings more complexities in safeguarding the private information.

Peter Wood, Chief Executive Officer of First Base Technologies LLP and a member of the ISACA London Chapter Security Advisory Group, explains that the crux of the issue is that big data's volume and velocity[7] "expands the boundaries of existing information security responsibilities and introduces significant new risks and challenges."[1]

Insufficiency of Privacy legislation

Limitation of existing code

There is no illustrative data protection structure in our country, however the limited and insufficient laws that are dealing with the protection of data are Information Technology Act, 2000 and Information Technology (Reasonable security practices &procedures & sensitive personal Data or information) Rules, 2011.

IT Act deal with the violation of an individual's right to privacy through digital means , however this act is not self sufficient to tackle repugnant increase in cyber crimes because of its provision being limited in scope. There have been amendments in the act and the new provisions are inserted but it could not provide for the efficiency of the existing act. With the changing dynamic, there have been explosion of new ways of committing crime through internet and this existing act being archaic could not get away with this growing menace of cyber crime.

Low conviction rate

Another loophole of this act is the worrying conviction rate over the years. According to National Crime Records Bureau report[8] there were total of 21,970 cases were registered from 2015 to 2020, however, the cases that went under trial were 382, out of which only 99 were convicted. These numbers are evident of the fact that there is no deterrence in the mind of people since the laws are not stringent enough that could create fear in the minds of people.

Delay in passing of Personal Data Protection Bill (PDPB)

In 2017, when the court pronounce judgment to declare privacy as a fundamental right gave rise to a hope that it would bring in an expressed legislation to govern data protection.

The Personal Data Protection Bill, which was the first active step towards the legislation of data privacy norms, was drafted in 2018, as a result of a committee headed by B.N Srikrishna[9], which deliberated upon the issue related to data protection and came up with this bill. This bill aims to achieve objective of providing security to the personal data of citizen by government and companies.

Moreover in 2019, this bill was submitted in Lok Sabha and was sent to Joint Parliamentary Committee for further deliberation. As of now, both the houses have granted fourth extension to Joint Parliamentary Committee[10] to submit its report on this bill, which is causing an indefinite delay for the bill to become an act and thus it has been 4 years and we have no codified law for the protection of right to privacy.

Recent cases of Data breaches in India

In the annual report of Indian Computer Emergency Response Team 2020[11], recorded 11,58,208 incidents of website intrusion & malware propagation, malicious code, ransom-ware attacks, data breaches & vulnerable security.

Till June 2021, more than 6.07 lakhs cases of cyber attacks were observed, and the leading cases of Dominos, Air India, Upstox, SBI, where the data of millions of customer were leaked from the database of company is a serious cause of concern for the government.

Although Section 43A of Information Technology Act,2000[12] provides for the responsibility of corporate bodies who are negligent in handling the sensitive personal data of its customers. Initially there was no specific definition of sensitive personal data under the IT Act, further the definition was given by the Information Technology (Reasonable security practices &procedures & sensitive personal Data or information) Rules, 2011. However, these rules have limitation that they apply only to body corporate and exclude the Government.

This make it even more necessary to expedite the process of Personal Data Protection Bill and make this an act, as this would govern all the public and private entities and would give more comprehensive definition of vague terms so as to provide for gaps in the existing code.

Conclusion

The legislation for privacy with respect to cyber space is still in its nascent stage and therefore, the Government has a key role to ensure that the rights of individuals are not intruded due to negligence.

Despite progress being made on enacting cyber laws and implementing them, cyber crime is still not nipped in the bud. Hence, Internet users need to be more careful of the sites they visit, know the privacy policy of these websites to protect their personal data as much as possible.

With the new technologies, hackers are also coming up with the new ways of committing crimes. There is need of amended legislation to accommodate the persistent and ever-changing threats to privacy in cyberspace. There is need of engaging with the private sector on the issue of cyber security implementation and privacy safeguards that still need to be strengthened.

Some suggestive measures to combat this threat-

- The PDPB, bill which is still under debate shall be passed expeditiously, which would eventually help in reducing increasing cases.
- The legislation shall be timely amended according to the changes taking place in the technology
- Government shall come up with more and more awareness campaigns so as to make citizen aware of the potential risks

Now, this is the need of an hour for Government to come up with stringent laws against this contagious disease of cybercrime which would uphold the right to privacy of an individual in this techno-savvy world.

CHAPTER TWELVE

RIGHT TO PRIVACY AND LEGALITY OF SURVEILLANCE

Author: Vrinda Chawla, II year of B.A.,LL.B.(Hons.) from UILS, Panjab University

CONCEPT OF PRIVACY

As the modern times began, many new concepts and doctrines emerged with the it. Notion of human life expanded far beyond the conventional ideas. It was realized that LIFE is not merely being alive, but it contains many other domains which make the human life meaningful. Some of which were recognized as life and death with dignity, having basic necessities of life fulfilled, having adequate Privacy etc. Privacy basically means having enough "private space", "the right to be alone" or "the state where one is free from public attention".

Article 21 of the Indian constitution provides every Indian citizen with a fundamental right, "Right to Life". In the post freedom era, graduallywith the development of Indian judiciary, the scope of right to life which crudely stood for just existing expanded to providing material meaning to people's lives. It began embracing several other components, including: Right to live with Dignity, right to basic nutrition requirement of human body, right to shelter etc. Walking down the same path, in 2017, in the landmark judgement of K.S PUTTASWAMY VS. UNION OF INDIA (WRIT PETITION CIVIL NO.494 OF 2012), it was held by the Apex court that RIGHT TO PRIVACY was a fundamental segment of right to life. This means that every Indian citizen has the right to maintain privacy of his life, his bodily integrity and personal autonomy. No one can cause hindrance to other person's right to enjoyment of his personal life in good faith. It is a kind of relationship between govt and people; between one person and others that no unwanted intrusion into the life of one would be caused unreasonably. Privacy has been considered very essential for the development of any given individual; it provides a way by which one can find his best self.

SURVEILLANCE AND IT'S LEGALITY

Surveillance stands for "close observation", of any individual or a body. Surveillance may be physical, digital, informative etc. With the growth of technology, the scope of surveillance has expanded beyond any limits. Every kind of data, personal conversations, administrative data etc., none is past the extent of surveillance, especially in the digital age. Every govt agency, statutory body or office is now well equipped with digital resources and is a storehouse of information of citizens, personal and governmental. The databases of these bodies contain data either collected through consensual forms, or though surveillance. In the Puttaswamy case, besides giving recognition to right to privacy, the apex court held that govt had full right and capability to hold all the required and legit information regarding citizens and their personal lives, whichever is essentially needed, as long as the same is adequately safeguarded by the govt. The center was directed to take appropriate measures to shelter the data so that no wrongdoing can occur. This ratifies that bounded surveillance by government is completely constitutional and legally upheld.

SOCIAL MEDIA APPS AND IMPACT ON PRIVACY

With the emergence of smart phones, social media applications have taken the dimensions of communication to another level. Apps like WhatsApp, Facebook, Instagram, Snapchat and innumerable more have shrunk the world. Availing these apps requires agreeing to certain terms and conditions which basically give the right to companies to store and use data of users, some even take permission of complete surveillance of personal conversations. The policies of social media apps have expanded the concept of surveillance to greatest boundaries. Studies have indicated that the private conversations, every action of users online can be easily tapped and recorded by the apps, the same being free to use it however they want, for commercial or marketing purposes. Social media apps can monitor information including location, relations of user and even his financial passcodes. This close monitoring of user data is surely endangering privacy, and more than privacy, it is endangering safety of the users.

The same has been highlighted by the supreme court of India in the latest judgement in the case of WhatsAppLLC vs Competition commission of

India &Anrs. (W.P C. 4378/2021 & CM 13336/2021)whereby the privacy policies of WhatsApp and Facebook were found to be jeopardizing user's Right to Privacy. The court ordered tech companies to disclose the purpose for which data will be used to the users before implementing the same. Value and grave concern over privacy was expressed by the courts as no real choice except AGREE is being given to users if they wish to continue using the app. Where alternates of WhatsApp and Facebook visibly don't exist, the use of these applications becomes necessity at some point. Legality of surveillance by these apps, at extreme level and depth, without even awareness of the user was questioned here.

The complication of surveillance by social media apps came into limelight specifically in greater proportion when the whole of human life shifted to virtual, from education to work, everything and anything which kept going even during the spread of deadly corona virus was only due the presence of internet and networking apps. The emergence of video calling apps which require permission to use camera have further increased the risk of unwanted surveillance, increasing concerns over privacy. Many questions arise here regarding legality of the same, where on one hand Indian judicial systems are giving so huge importance to the same and working effortlessly to protect the fundamental Right to Privacy, where are social media apps and blameworthy huge surveillance taking us on the other hand?

INITIATIVES BY GOI TO SAFEGUARD RIGHT TO PRIAVCY

Steadily widening distress over matters of privacy has urged the govt to take some steps to ensure safety of citizens. One of the earliest attempts by center was releasing Privacy Protection Bill, 2011. The crux of this bill was that "Every person has a right to protection of his personal data and legal information passed on through telephonic conversations or use of any other electronic media, which are important to save his honor and family life". An important point to be noted here is that when this bill was passed, in the year 2011, telephones were the bulk means of communication as internetworking was not highly developed. Such attempts depict that how privacy forms the very foundation of our ideals.

The latest Data protection bill, 2019, later named as Data protection bill, 2021 even thoughstands on the pillars of protecting and safeguarding privacy, pictures many shortcomings. Full and final right of surveillance, even mass access to personal communication has been declared valid by this bill, if it falls into ensuring the interest and security of state. The govt hasput this bill supreme to all other legislations in the same field. The very soul of this bill which was supposed to be "protection of privacy of citizens" is now revolving around "maintaining state security". More than serving its purpose, the bill seems to have been providing the govt with more and more power to intrigue and encroach personal lives of people in the name of "states' interest". The most decried feature of this act is the power of exemption given to the govt whereby the same can exempt any govt agency or statutory body's surveillance of personal data under certain given conditions. Now the question here arises that when a bill which is supposed to preserve the heart of Article 21, Right to Privacy, is instead saving the state's right to intervene in personal communication and data, then how exactly is Indian legislative system going to fulfil the ideas upon which our country and its constitution stand?

Another recent watershed event in the ongoing chronology of surge in surveillance is the revelation of spy software "Pegasus". Pegasus is a software developed by Israeli tech company NSO group with the major purpose of helping world govts to keep an eye on terrorists, criminals and antisocial element, so that better governance can take place. Another important factor contributing to the development of Pegasus software is the concern that concept of privacy, which is to help people live a better life, should not conversely be used as a shield by negative elements to top off their convictions. This software is only available to govts and can be used in law enforcement and counterterrorism work, but in the year 2021, disclosures have been made regarding use of this software to spy upon journalists, protesters, politicians and other influential people by govts of over 50 countries. The technology of software has developed to such a level that the person being spied won't be able to detect the presence of Pegasus in his smartphone by any means! Studies have indicated the use of this software by Indian govt as well, to spy upon abovementioned gentry. Here, many questions arise regarding approach of center towards the fundamental rights of people. This surveillance not only obstructs the Right to privacy, but its legality is also questionable under many acts of India including Information technology act which put this kind of surveillance into unlawful bracket.

CONCLUSION

After a really long wrestle since independence, Indian citizens were finally presented a right which was indeed requisite at this point of time, the Right to Privacy. This fact can't be denied that Article 21 i.e. Right to Life would inevitably be lifeless and mundane if it did not consist vitality of providing privacy. Of course, how can anyone flourish and blossom if he can't see a private and personal life of his own, which is free from any unwanted monitoring and inspection? The value of this right is well recognized by citizens. Privacy forms the very foundation of a human life, and thus, it should be guarded and preserved by every means the state has.

With the technology developing and means of creating chaos in a society increasing, surveillance becomes necessary at a certain point. But the fine line that exists between necessity of surveillance and infringement to people's privacy should be well respected. Nonetheless, where mechanism of surveillance is increasing on one side of the coin, the other side is still questioning the legality and extent of surveillance. The terminal beyond which any surveillance would harm Right to Privacy is still a dubiety. Thus, it can be concluded that attempts to find the precise balance between both the sides of this coin should continue until we find an equilibrium.

CHAPTER THIRTEEN

WOMEN'S MARRIAGE AGE TO BE RAISED TO 21

Author: Ayushi Tomar, II year of B.A.,LL.B.

Ayushi Tomar

The news

The union cabinet has approved a major reform., and nonetheless it is finally happening.The Union Cabinet has cleared the proposal of raising the minimum age for women from 18 years to 21. Presently, the minimum age of marriage for women is 18 and 21 for men. The government will now look to introduce amendments to the Prohibition of Child Marriage Act, Special Marriage Act, and the Hindu Marriage Act to bring the plan into action.

"To save the daughters from malnutrition, it is necessary that they are married at the right age," Modi had said. Raising the age for women is a good move towards women empowerment and ensuring women are on equal footing with men in keeping with the vision of the Constitution on gender equality.

An Insight

The raise of marriage is a good start. In India, marriages before 18 are so common, and we are not talking about high school love marriages but forced marriages. They happen all over India. Families eagerly wait to turn their daughters 18, and when they do, they're made to marry without giving them any other option. They are made to sacrifice their study and asked to start a family, with no financial independence, no freedom, no second other options, and with no experience. They are impregnated soon after, which sometimes results in premature deliveries and sometimes the death of the mother. She is pushed into a relationship that she may or may not want.Early marriage brings early pregnancies with massive health consequences, complications, and mental health problems.

Is an 18-year-old equipped to deal with all of these? India has always been a patriarchal society and the culture of hypergamy has always been prevalent. There has always been a disparity between women and men.

The Backlashes

But now, there are always some critics. Here's what they ask:

" What difference do 3 years make? If you're forced to pay dowry at 18 or you are forced into a relationship at 18, you will be forced to do this at 21."

But here is what I have to say... STOP THINKING FROM A MAN'S PERSPECTIVE OR THE FAMILY'S PERSPECTIVE. THINK FROM A WOMAN'S PERSPECTIVE FOR A CHANGE. In 3 years she could complete her education... in 3 years, she could get a job... and in 3 years SHE WOULD PROBABLY FIGHT AND REJECT MEN WHO ASK FOR DOWRY. That is what real progress looks like.

Opposition parties said the proposed legislation was written in "haste," without adequate consultations, and is an attack on the laws of religious communities. Women's organizations and gender and legal experts said it goes against the international norm of 18 as the minimum marriage age and takes away sexual and marital freedom of choice for people who are otherwise legally adults.

But let these critics be shown a pragmatic approach.Women have never been allowed to enjoy their liberty effectively. In the rural areas, they are denied proper education either due to the non-availability of resources or they are pushed into household works because of the common belief,"women belong to the kitchen." They are married off as soon as they reach puberty and are made prey to domestic violence and marital rape. As far as sexual freedom is concerned, people be reminded of the fact that it is not illegal to have a physical relationship before marriage as far as the person involved is major.

Women centric reforms bring holistic changes

Just think about what you have at 18? No degree, a little understanding plus you have just exited the most volatile period of your life, your teenage. Most parents think of their daughters as a mouth to feed; and how do you eliminate that mouth? The answer is "by marrying her off."

This means the reform should not end here. Raising the minimum age is step 1. Step 2 is outreach and awareness. Make sure girls are put in schools... make sure they get the same meals as their brothers and make sure there is no social stigma of marrying late.

Modern society states that it is a woman's choice to decide whether to get married or stay single or when to marry. But the fact is most women in India are denied choices. So the higher legal age is the only solution. In fact, it could be a new template for governance in India, reforms that target women.

We have seen so many examples in this country like the abolition of the triple talaq. It was an archaic tradition that had no place in the 21st century. Women-centric reforms bring holistic change and it is a fact. Former Indian Prime Minister has said, " if you educate a man, you educate an individual... However, if you educate a woman, you educate a family."

The fact is, when women take the lead, the reforms work out better. Raising a woman's age is a good idea but we must do more. We must offer more opportunities for Indian women. Force must be on creating social awareness about women's reproductive health, their individual rights, making them realize to be assertive, educating them and empowering them, or else.... WE WILL NOT ERADICATE FORCED MARRIAGES, WE WILL JUST HAVE DELAYED THEM.

CHAPTER FOURTEEN

JUVIENILE DELINQUENCY IN INDIA – LATEST AMENDMENTS IN JUVENILE JUSTICE

Author: Nancy Maggo, IV year of B.B.A.,LL.B.(Hons.) from Law College Dehradun faculty of Uttaranchal University

Nancy Maggo

ABSTRACT

Adolescent misconduct is a not kidding offenses and its hindering for the social request in any country. There is a patterns of expansions in adolescent violations world-over, with increasingly more contribution of the young in rough wrongdoings. India shows comparative patterns of expanding pace of abuses wrongdoings committed by the adolescents .It is an intense worry for the country and answer for end the issue should be looked for cautiously .Indian overall set of laws and legal executive has reacted to these patterns and has acquired a few corrections the laws relating to adolescent equity in India. This paper target taking a gander at the reasons for adolescent misconduct and clarifications given by researchers from different fields to clarify the issue. The investigation of measurable information accessible at true destinations demonstrates expanding association of the adolescents in appealing wrongdoings to contain the issue of Juvenile Delinquency in India. The Act relating to Juvenile Delinquency has been corrected and presently trail of adolescents engaged with grievous violations is held as grown-ups.

INTRODUCTION

A Latin proverb that suits best for the adolescent equity framework in India is 'Nothing Novi Spectrum' which infers that nothing is new on this planet .There has existed an assumption in the entire world since the antiquated period that the adolescent ought to be managed indulgently in light of the fact that there exists an arrangement of thought that says-Young folks for the most part have a propensity to react in a genuine and delayed dissatisfaction which is went with forceful methodologies.

Over the most recent couple of years, it is additionally seen that the wrongdoings done by kids younger than 15-16 have expanded fundamentally .The overall inclination or the brain research behind the responsibility of the wrongdoing or the reasons for wrongdoing are early-valuable encounters, dominate manliness, upbringing, economic ruins, absence of training, and so on It involves lowness that the youngsters younger than 6-10 are these days utilized as instruments for Carrying out unlawful or criminal operations. Since the personalities of the children have a guiltless and manipulative person, they can be baited at a small expense.

Preceding the adolescent equity demonstration of 2015, 2000 and 1986, there existed the youngsters demonstration of 1960 that meant to give impacts to the worldwide responses towards the issue of Juvenile Justice by which they gave a uniform approach that ensured the interests and privileges of an adolescent and that took a gander at care, treatment, recovery and improvement of a kid fundamentally.

In any case, with the new improvements in the global local area and ensuing rise of the contribution of adolescents in wrongdoing, the Indian officials are completed to come forward with new, moderate and stricter laws for the concerned adolescent framework in the nation. Subsequently ,the adolescent equity demonstration of 1986 and afterward adolescent equity demonstration of 2015 was passed by the parliament.

When previous boss equity if India, equity V.K Krishna Iyer expressed that we really want correctional code in light of the fact that the youngster is the dad of man and assuming we're disregarding the underdevelopment in kids, then, at that point, we would be at fault for some shortcomings and blunders connected with leaving our kids.

Over the most recent couple of many years, the crime percentage by the kids under age of 16 years has expanded , the explanation of expanding crime percentage is might be because of the childhood climate of the kid , monetary condition , absence of schooling and the parental consideration . these are the a portion of the fundamental explanation .and the most baffling part is that , youngsters (particularly under the age gathering of 5 to 7 years)now a days are utilized as apparatus for committing the wrongdoing as at that this stage their psyche is extremely guiltless and can undoubtedly be controlled.

MEANING AND POINTS OF JUVENILE JUSTICE

An Adolescent is a youngster who isn't yet developed to the point of being considered to be an adult. Adolescent equity deals with the treatment of children in the battle with the law and moreover looks at the principle drivers of guilty lead and measures to deflect such direct.

POINT OF JUVENILE JUSTICE

- It depends on the freedoms of the kid
- It applies the standards of supportive equity i.e to reestablish the equilibrium of circumstance upset by wrongdoing rather than basically allotting discipline.
- This framework puts the wellbeing of the youngster first.
- The essential target of this framework is to zero in on the avoidance of wrongdoings and shamefulness done to the adolescents.

WHAT IS JUVENILE DELINQUENCY

Adolescent misconduct is the involvement of a child who is between the age of 10 and 17 in criminal behavior or behavior.

Juvenile unfortunate behavior is similarly used to imply young person who is show consistent direct of mischief or rebelliousness, to be considered out of parental control, becoming obviously liable to authentic movement by the court system. Adolescent misconduct is otherwise called ' Juvenile Offering', and each state has a different overall set of laws set up to manage adolescents who overstep the law.

WHO ARE JUVENILE DELIQUENTS?

Adolescent Delinquent are routinely youth between the ages of 10 and 17 who have completed a criminal exhibit. There are two chief kinds of liable gatherings: repeat miscreants and age specific liable gatherings.

- Repeat Wrongdoers – go over blameworthy gatherings are generally called ' life course steady miscreants.' These juvenile reprobates start chargeable or alluding to other lone lead in the midst of pre-adulthood. Go over liable gatherings continue to take part in criminal activities or powerful practices even later they enter adulthood.
- Age – specific liable gatherings Age-explicit wrongdoers show juvenile criminal direct beginnings in the midst of energy. Not in the least like the repeat transgressors, regardless, the acts of the age – specific liable party close before the minor transforms into adults.

On account of Gopinath Ghosh v. Province of West Bengal, the denounced had given his age as much over the remove age endorsed for being a kid. In any case, for this situation , the court not just permitted the supplication of kid status to be raised interestingly yet additionally alluded the make a difference to the age of the charged. Supporting this methodology, the Supreme Court in Rajinder Chandra v. Province of Chhattisgarh , further set out that the norm of confirmation for age assurance is the level of likelihood and not verification without question.

JUSTIFICATIONBEHIND JUVENILE CRIMES

Interdisciplinary investigations on adolescents misconduct uncover that across the world, numerous conduct changes happen in the adolescents/ juvenile , which are connected with the unexpected changes in their body due hormonal flood, related with pubescence .The progressions are generally evident in actual boundaries, like change in stature and weight of the teenagers, and are before long followed by other sexual and actual changes of development .these actual changes are accompanied by mental changes moreover.

SOCIAL FACTORS

Some of the time, the adolescents foster delinquent sub – culture because of social hardship and status disappointment that they go through (Albert Cohen,1955) .they regularly take on the delinquent propensities because of friend pressure. As per Walter B. Mill operator ,some adolescent (for the most part having a place with lower class) turn the standard culture upside down , subsequently whatever is esteemed and is viewed as sure by and large by the is society surrendered these young, and is supplanted by the polar opposite esteem framework . consequently, assuming specific ethics are maintained by society , adolescent reprobates surrender these qualities and attempt to dominate in the space of sturdiness, over-hurting the others and enjoy things that give them energy (characterized as central worries by mill operator). Delinquent sub – culture hypothesis has been applied in most recent examinations in the US, where new space of mentality of the adolescent towards the police in china has been engaged.

MENTAL FACTORS

There are mental clarification to misconduct additionally, which can be surely known through Freudian ideas of id, inner self and super-inner self. At the point when the id (the instinctual component person's character) turns out to be too solid and the super inner self becomes frail the self image forms into hostile to social individual. There can a solid connection between detainees in Bangladesh showed exceptionally high frequency of mental problem among the wrongdoers of female adolescent place. These guilty parties additionally showed high rate of substance misuse.

NATURAL FACTORS

The natural clarification recommand that people are affected by their organic/hereditary make up. They are not by and large the hostages of natural planning, but rather it delivers these people leaned towards delinquent propensities. The hormonal changes in the body of the adolescents are liable for their incautious and defiant conduct. Biological/ natural and monetary boundaries additionally play significant trigger focuses in existences of the adolescents . yet, as a rule it's the blend of these variables that together causes circumstance of adolescent wrongdoing.

ADVANCEMENT OF JUVENILE JUSTICE LEGISLATION IN INDIA

A few creators have assessed the origin and advancement of adolescent judges in India .Prior to happening to British in India, the activities of youngsters were represented under existing Hindu and Muslim laws , where the individual groups of the individual concerned were considered liable for observing the activities of their kids. In India , the requirement for new regulations for kids was felt under the English rule. Some particular laws were passed somewhere in the range of 1850 and 1919 , like the student act (1850), the code of criminal method (1861) and the reformatory school act (1867 and 1897).

Under the understudy act 1850 , it was held that desperate or unimportant wrongdoers in the age gathering of 10 to 18 years ought to be managed independently – the sentenced youngsters were needed to fill in as disciples for financial specialists. Area 82 of the Indian corrective code of 1860 likewise perceived the unique status of kids. It put forth age lines on criminal obligation and avoided youngsters more youthful than 7 from culpability. The kids between 7 to 12 years old were considered to have adequate development to comprehend the idea of their activities under particular conditions.

The code of criminal method of 1861 took into account separate path assuming people more youthful that age 15 and their treatment under the reformatories rather than detainment facilities. It additionally set down arrangements of probation of the youthful guilty parties.

The adolescent equity (care and security) act was passed in 2000. It accommodated a uniform legitimate system of equity the nation over . the fundamental target of the new demonstration was to guarantee that no kid (up to the age 18 years) guilty party is stopped in prison. The demonstration additionally made arrangement for the foundation and apparatus care , security ,recovery of youngsters . the demonstration was again altered in 2006 and afterward in 2010.

The adolescent equity act, separated for giving fir care, assurance, recovery and advancement needs additionally makes the adolescent settling and attitude framework kid well disposed .it empowers the adolescent equity board (prior called adolescent court) in adopting a multi-disciplinary strategy when directing asks. Under the demonstration , youngster government assistance board of trustees has been set up to take into account needs of weak kids. New demonstration managing adolescent misconduct came in 2015, regarding which a conversation will be held later in this article.

ADOLESCENT CRIMES IN INDIA : INVOLVING MINORS THAT SHOOK INDIA

Barot house is a zee5 original film featuring Amit Sadh, Manjari Fadnnes and Aaryan menghgi motivated by genuine occasion, the story rotates around the cherishing barot family whose bliss is fleeting later their girl is seen as fiercely killed in the house, under puzzling conditions. The story includes adolescents wrongdoing, accordingly we have gone along adolescent wrongdoing cases including minors that shook India .

1. Nirbhaya Gang Rape- In 2012 Delhi assault and deadly attack is broadly realized milestone case that prompted changes in the Indian legal executive framework. One of the attackers for the situation was a minor.
2. Minor kills sibling over PUBG – PUBG has been an ongoing theme tying a few criminal cases across the world that occurred as of late. A 15 years kid supposedly banged his senior sibling's head on the divider and assaulted him with scissors later he requested that he quit playing the game.
3. The homicide of Tik Tok VIP – two or three months prior, there adolescents were captured in the homicide of tik tok big name , was shoot dead in a bustling Delhi market.

NEED FOR AMENDMENT IN JUVENILE JUSTICE

Because of this pattern, lawful meaning of youngster under Indian overall set of laws went under question. Malvika Tyagi 2016 likewise feels that with pattern of association of adolescents in violet wrongdoings in India, state mediation is needed as far as making alterations and in wording getting new arrangement. The new adolescent equity demonstration of 2015 took into comprehension the association of adolescents in horrifying wrongdoings and drew out certain alterations. Under the new lawful arrangements, if an offspring of 16 years or above carries out an appalling wrongdoing, a fundamental appraisal of his psychological and actual development will be made by the adolescent equity board.

The adolescent equity bill was presented in the Lok Sabha in 2014, later it was felt in the past Nirbhaya case that some move must be made against the expanding inclusion of adolescents in the age gathering of 16 to 18 in offensive/genuine violations.

The bill presented ideas from Hauge show on security of youngsters and participation in regard of between country reception 1993. It was set down under the bill of 2015 that the adolescent equity board will choose whether an adolescent wrongdoer in the age gathering of 16 to 18 years ought to be treat as a grown-up. Those adolescents who perpetrate horrifying violations such homicide and assault (which welcomes discipline of 7 years or more) ought to be treated as grown-ups. Anyway , assuming the board chooses , the adolescent can be sent for restoration.

ADOLESCENT DELINQUENCY IN INDIA – CURRENT TENDS

The lawful meaning of kid influences how the courts in a nation manages guilty parties. According to the worldwide standards , and furthermore under the adolescent equity framework in India, a minor or a youngster can't be attempted in a similar way as a grown-up. A kid is treated as Doli Incapax, without any, Mens-rea he/she isn't fit for understanding outcomes of his/her activities.

Remembering this rationale, kids are managed under adolescent equity framework , and not under the grown-up criminal equity framework. They can never be given detainment or capital punishment. Subsequently , under the Indian overall set of laws, craftsmanship. 40 (3) (a) of CRC requires state gatherings to advance foundation of least age beneath which youngster is assumed not to have ability to stray the reformatory law. Period of criminal obligation is held to be 7 years-kid under 7 years can't be viewed as a kid in struggle with law – segment 82 of IPC ,1860. In this way , nothing is an offense done by kid somewhere in the range of 7 and 12 years , who has not achieved adequate development to pass judgment on the nature and outcomes of his/her direct , and didn't realize that what s/he was doing was wrong – area 83 of IPC , 1860.

Be that as it may, adolescent misconduct has been expanding in capital city Delhi and different spots in India at a disturbing rate. The contribution of the adolescents in genuine offenses like homicide, endeavor to murder, seizing and kidnapping has brought worries up in the country. Later the December 2012 assault in Delhi (or Nirbhaya case, as it was normally called), many discussions and conversations highlighted the gentler methodologies of adolescent equity framework to genuine offenses.

The National Crime Records Bureau (NCRB) information indicates that there has been an expansion in wrongdoings committed by adolescents , particularly by those in the 16-18 years age bunch. NCRB information given underneath shows the patterns of adolescent offenses.

CONCLUSION

The adolescent equity demonstration of 2016 should be visible as an exceptionally moderate advance of the Indian government towards staying up with changing patterns in adolescent violations. The intense advance under the follow up on treating the adolescent wrongdoers viewed as at real fault for carrying out intolerable wrongdoing as grown-ups, dependent upon the perceptions of the adolescent equity board . the Justice Verma panel stood firm against the bringing down of the period of adolescents in struggle with law . it was seen in the report that ' any endeavor of diminishing the period of adolescence, or barring specific kids from the review of the adolescent equity (Care and Protection of kids) act 2000 based on nature of the offense and age, will abuse guarantees made under the constitution and worldwide instruments , the unified country show of freedoms of the kid(UNCR)

Be that as it may, the high court in India took stand in opposition to the idea and cautioning of the advisory group . it was contended that the age of 18 years was fixed in light of the master thought of therapists that youngsters/adolescent up to this age are pliant and can be improved through reclaiming and reestablishing techniques. it was then contended that putting them with grown-up hoodlums would re-mingle them into the universe of wrongdoing and convert them into no-nonsense lawbreakers.

It is to be remembered that the lawful sub-framework is a piece of the bigger social framework. Any adjustment of the bigger entire, that is the general public requires changes in the constituent parts or the more modest sub – sub framework. hence , when changes are happening in the general public at a high speed , the overall set of laws needs to go in a state of harmony with the general public. The adolescent equity (care and insurance) act 2015 has brought these changes.

Author's Bio

Nancy maggo student of BBALLB (Hons.) From Law College Dehradun faculty of Uttaranchal University.

CHAPTER FIFTEEN

CRYPTOCURRENCY RISE CONCERN: INDIAN LAWS IN THE NEW DIGITAL CURRENCY ERA

Author: Aditya Yadav, I year of B.B.A.,LL.B.(Hons.) from the Northcap University

Aditya Yadav

Bitcoin is mostly about anonymous transaction, and I don't think over time that's a good way to go. I'm a huge believe in digital currency...but doing it on an anonymous basis I think that leads to some abuses, so I'm not involved in bitcoin.

- Bill Gates

Cryptocurrency is gaining popularity in the past few years and rapidly increasing day by day in India and the rest of the world. Cryptocurrency is digital money created from code and works on blockchain technology which is an encrypted string of data or a hash, encoded to signify one unit of currency.

In Indian cryptocurrency is seen as an investment way rather than used as a currency for purchasing commodities. In Indian only there are above 10 cr. Crypto owners in the world followed by the United States of America and Russia.

The main reasons for the rise of crypto in India in the last few years are various failed government policies and fewer returns and low-rate development resulting in disillusionment with the banking system and progressive taxation and further leading investments in cryptocurrency.

In 2017, a committee comprising FinMin, RBI and SEBI members is formed to look at the regulation over the assent. Two PIL'S were filed against the use of cryptocurrency in the Supreme Court of India.

On April 6, 2018, the RBI issues a circular banning all financial entities from dealing with any entity dealing in cryptocurrencies. After that, the Internet and mobile association of India and other petitioners had challenged the circular by arguing that it had put an end to the industry by taking it out of the formal economy, even though there is no ban on cryptocurrencies in the country.

In March 2020, the Supreme court bench quashed the central bank's circulation on grounds of disproportionality. The judgment noted that the RBI has failed to show at least some semblance of any damage suffered by its regulated entities, to back its decision to effectively bar cryptocurrencies in India.

In 2021, the government says it will introduce a bill to create a sovereign digital currency and simultaneously ban all private cryptocurrencies. It was listed as Cryptocurrency and Regulation of official Digital Currency Bill,2021 for introduction budget session but it was not brought in the parliament.

In the present-day scenario through various sources, it is said that the government of India is in a thinking mode whether to ban cryptocurrency or not.

Dangerous impacts of cryptocurrency

- As cryptocurrencies have the potential to change the world for the better but at the same time they can be used to facilitate criminal enterprises such as money laundering schemes, direct trafficking and even terrorism. Terrorist groups have been interested in crypto because it enables almost instant transfers of money across borders without the oversight of central authority since terrorists are locked out of the traditional financial system they have been testing Bitcoin as an alternative way to fund their activities and are a sustainable source of funding for terrorists and it gives a real advantage to the terrorists as they can receive an unlimited amount of money from everywhere in the world by accepting Bitcoin however once they receive their Bitcoin they are likely to have a hard time managing and spending those fund. So, terrorists need to cash out this means they need to rely on some sort of centralising infrastructure such as a cryptocurrency exchange. Terrorist groups like ISIS are raising their funds for more than two years and raised more than hundreds of thousands of dollars worth of bitcoins also because the Bitcoin price went up this time they call their supporters to donate the organization with Bitcoin from different means like websites. One of the many jihadi groups fighting in the serial civil war was also asking for Bitcoin donations on Twitter and they did not publish the article address but the doors were up to send a direct message to more information on how to donate. Cryptocurrencies are far from being a prominent source of funding for terrorism but still, blockchain technology is evolving and terrorists are learning fast which means regulators and companies shouldn't ignore this potential threat coming shortly.

- As per the article by The Guardian, it states that "IMF warns of global risks from unregulated cryptocurrency boom" and greater financial instability, fraud, and funding of terrorism likely unless government toughen supervision, the fund says.[1]As cryptocurrency is deregulated, a peer-to-peer economy and decentralized and can increase the risk of cyber frauds and thief. It is not fully secure and a gateway for spoofing, hacking, fake initial coin offering (ICO) etc.

- Cryptocurrencies are very volatile and unstable.

<u>**Current scenario**</u>

The government will introduce the new Crypto Bill in Parliament after Cabinet approval, Union Finance Minister Nirmala Sitharaman said on November 30[2]. The finance minister also said that regulation of NFTs (non-fungible tokens) is also being discussed by the Centre. Speaking during Question Hour in Rajya Sabha, the Finance Minister said, "We are close to bringing a bill in parliament. It will be introduced in the house once the cabinet clears the bill." Sitharaman said the new Bill has come up after reworking on the old Bill that could not be tabled in previous sessions of Parliament. She said that the risk that cryptocurrencies can lead to undesirable activities is also being closely monitored. No decision was taken on banning the advertisements published on different cryptocurrency platforms. However, steps will be taken to create awareness.

Conclusion

If the government would not ban cryptocurrency, then a proper regulation and centralisation of the transaction should be there. Misleading ads regarding a cryptocurrency should be monitored by the Advertisement Standard Council of India (ASCI) and awareness should be circulated by the government regarding the risks involved and volatility in cryptocurrency.

Consumer protection act should be made into consideration like SEBI which is a very successful body that monitors investments in the stock market and the person is protected. Money laundering and issues like terror financing should be strictly monitored and stopped by making suitable schemes and actions made by the government.

CHAPTER SIXTEEN

DISHA RAVI TOOLKIT CASE : WAS IT SEDITIOUS?

Author: Shubham Ranjan, II year of B.A.,LL.B.(Hons.) from School Of Law, Bennett University, The Times of India Group

Shubham Ranjan

Background of the issue

Disha Ravi is an environmental activist who holds a degree of Bachelor in Business Administration from a college in Bengaluru. The 21-year-old environment extremist is likewise one of the establishing individuals from a gathering named 'Fridays For Future India'.[1]

The capture of a 21-year-old environment dissident for her supposed association with her inclusion in the Greta Thunberg tool compartment case has started cross country shock. The environment lobbyist was captured from her home in North Bengaluru on Saturday for purportedly imparting to Greta Thunberg the "tool stash" identified with the rancher's dissent against the Center's three homestead laws. The Delhi Police alleged that Disha Ravi was an editorial manager of the "toolbox Google doc" and "key plotter" in the record's plan and spread. Police likewise claimed that Disha Ravi and others "teamed up with supportive of Khalistani Poetic Justice Foundation to spread alienation against the Indian State."

The Delhi Police claimed in a tweet that she was the person who was alleged to have shared the toolbox with Greta Thunberg. Greta Thunberg is a Sweden based adolescent environment extremist who had shared the "toolkit" in support of the farmers protest against the three homestead change laws. In the record, different instant activities, including making a Twitter storm and fighting external Indian embassies all across the globe, were recorded which should have been taken to help the farmers protest. The toolkit has been referred to by certain pundits as "confirmation" of her intrigue to fuel synchronous protests all across the country. Disha Ravi was presented before the watchful eyes of a Delhi court on the fourteenth day of February 2020 and was granted remand for police custody for five days. The police argued in the court that Disha's remand was the need of the hour as they are predicting a bigger intrigue against the Government of India and to discover her active roles and connections with the Khalistan movement. The case against Disha and the co-accused, a Mumbai based lawyer, Nikita Jacob and Pune based Engineer Shantanu Muluk has been lodged under sections 124(a) (Sedition), 153(a) which is for the promotion of enmity among various groups and 120(b) which is for Criminal Conspiracy of the Indian penal code.

What Is Sedition?

If some individual lures people of the country to rebel against the state authorities through his or her Acts or Speeches is considered to be a Seditious act. As in the present case, the accused have also been charged under this section. If we proceed further with the definition of the Sedition Law Under Section 124A of the Indian Penal Code “Whoever, by words, either spoken or written, or by signs, or by visible representation, or otherwise, brings or attempts to bring into hatred or contempt, or excites or attempts to excite disaffection towards the Government established by law shall be punished with imprisonment for life, to which fine may be added, or with imprisonment which may extend to three years, to which fine may be added, or with fine.”[3]

Therefore, the Delhi Police claims that the arrest of the accused is lawful as they intended to excite a feeling of disaffection against the "Government Established by the Law". It can be inferred that this Law has been used as a tool by various Governments against the critics of the Government and it is also expected to be the same in this case as well. The Britishers brought this act in the nineteenth century to Crush the rebellions and revolts against the Crown and the Government of the United Kingdom and the same law has been copied in our system as well. However, when the Indian Penal Code was written in the year 1861, this section was not included there and this is the reason why it is being written as section 124A, not 124. It was after the Wahabi revolt after which this section got added to the IPC. This Law was used for the first time in the year 1897 against Bal Gangadhar Tilak as he was alleged to have written against the British Raj at that time. Later, during the freedom struggle, it was used against many freedom fighters irrespective of the amount of violence they used at that point of time, in fact even after Mahatma Gandhi due to his critical writings against the Britishers. The validity of this law has also been challenged several times. Immediately after the Independence in 1951, the Punjab High Court gave a judgement declaring this Law to be Unconstitutional as it was considered by the court to be violative of Article 19 (1) (a) of the Constitution Of India.

There was an appeal filed in the Apex Court and by a Constitutional bench, this Provision was upheld in the year 1962. The case was Kedarnath Singh vs. State of Bihar[4] where the court looked into the matter as to whether this Law is synchronous to the fundamental right to speech and expression under Article 19 (1)(a)[5]. Here in this case the Supreme Court gave directions that "every citizen of the country owns a right to speech either written or spoken against the Government till the extent it does not" intice people to violence" against a lawfully assigned government. Though the Judgement upheld the Constitutionality of the Law, still the application of the law has been limited to "acts involving intention or tendency to create disorder, or disturbance of law and order, or incitement to violence." Here, concerning the Disha Ravi Case as of now, there is no sign or representation which would state their acts Seditious according to the freedom of Speech and Expression.

CONCLUSION

In conclusion, over the years this law has been used as a tool to harass the critics of the Government. If we go with some facts then the Jharkhand Government has accused more than ten thousand farmers belonging to the tribal communities of land acquisition projects.

Author's Bio

The author, Shubham Ranjan is presently pursuing BALLB (2nd Year) from the School of Law, Bennett University, The Times of India Group. He shows keen interest in writing about the socio-legal issues.

9 798885 556477

Printed by Libri Plureos GmbH in Hamburg,
Germany